Geomythology

Gold-guarding griffins, Cyclopes, killer lakes, human-eating birds, and "fire devils" from the sky—such wonders have long been dismissed as fictional. Now, thanks to the richly interdisciplinary field of geomythology, researchers are taking a second look. It turns out that these and similar tales, which originated in pre-literate societies, contain surprisingly accurate, pre-scientific intuitions about startling or catastrophic earth-based phenomena such as volcanoes, earthquakes, tsunamis, and the unearthing of bizarre animal bones. *Geomythology: How Common Stories Reflect Earth Events* provides an accessible, engaging overview of this hybrid discipline. The introductory chapter surveys geomythology's remarkable history and its core concepts, while the second and third chapters analyze the geomythical resonances of universal earth tales about dragons and giants. Chapter 4 narrows the focus to regional stories and discusses the ways these and other myths have influenced legends about griffins, Cyclopes, and other iconic creatures. The final chapter considers future avenues of research in geomythology, including geohazard management, geomythology databases, geomythical "cold cases," and ways the discipline might eventually set, rather than merely support, research agendas in science. Thus, the book constitutes a valuable asset for scientists and lay readers alike, particularly in a time of growing interest in monsters, massive climate change, and natural disasters.

Timothy J. Burbery received his Ph.D. in English, English Renaissance Literature, from Stony Brook University, in 1997. He is currently Professor of English at Marshall University, where he teaches, among other subjects, Shakespeare, scientific and technical writing, science fiction, and ecocriticism/literary theory.

Routledge Focus on Literature

On Lingering and Literature
Harold Schweizer

The Rise of the Australian Neurohumanities
Conversations Between Neurocognitive Research and Australian Literature
Edited by Jean-François Vernay

Neo-Georgian Fiction
Re-imagining the Eighteenth Century in the Contemporary Historical Novel
Edited by Jakub Lipski and Joanna Maciulewicz

Introduction to Digital Humanities
Enhancing Scholarship with the Use of Technology
Kathryn C. Wymer

Geomythology
How Common Stories Reflect Earth Events
Timothy J. Burbery

Re-Reading the Eighteenth-Century Novel
Studies in Reception
Jakub Lipski

Trump and Autobiography
Corporate Culture, Political Rhetoric, and Interpretation
Nicholas K. Mohlmann

For more information about this series, please visit: https://www.routledge.com/Routledge-Focus-on-Literature/book-series/RFLT

Geomythology
How Common Stories Reflect Earth Events

Timothy J. Burbery

Routledge
Taylor & Francis Group

NEW YORK AND LONDON

First published 2021
by Routledge
605 Third Avenue, New York, NY 10017

and by Routledge
2 Park Square, Milton Park, Abingdon, Oxon, OX14 4RN

*Routledge is an imprint of the Taylor & Francis Group, an
informa business*

Library of Congress Cataloging-in-Publication Data
A catalog record for this title has been requested

ISBN 13: 978-0-367-71106-1 (hbk)
ISBN 13: 978-0-367-71109-2 (pbk)

Typeset in Times New Roman
by MPS Limited, Dehradun

Contents

Illustrations

Acknowledgments

Since geomythology is one of the most interdisciplinary of fields, I am considerably indebted to experts in areas outside my own specialities (literature and literary theory). The following reviewers were unfailingly generous with their time and comments as I worked to get the science right: Aley El-Shazly (geology), Duane Hamacher (astronomy), and Nick Freidin (archaeology). Thanks are due, as well, to my Routledge editor Michelle Salyga for her encouragement in the project's early stages. I am also heavily indebted to folklorist-historian Adrienne Mayor, geomythographer extraordinaire, whose remarkable work in this area sparked my initial interest in the subject. Her comments on this manuscript have been invaluable, and any remaining errors or shortcomings are, of course, my own. Finally, thanks to my wife Hannah for her support throughout the writing of the book.

Introduction: What Is Geomythology?

Throughout history, there have been many famous battles and wars in which, for hours, days, months, even years, neither side was able to gain the upper hand. Among these are the Vietnam War, the Korean War, the Battle of Verdun (in World War I), the Battle of Waterloo, and the Siege of Leningrad (in World War II). Yet before all these events, there was the Titanomachy. The mother of all stalemated conflicts, it featured the upstart Olympians against their forebears: the Titans. It dragged on for ten years, with no clear victor. Finally, Zeus, the All-Father, enlisted the help of the Cyclopes and the so-called "Hundred-handers" (Greek: *Gyges*), springing both groups from Tartarus where they had been imprisoned by their father, Uranus. When the two armies readied for battle yet again, the Gyges were holding massive rocks in their many hands—and Zeus was packing Cyclopean lightning and thunder.

However, the Titans had not been idle during the hiatus. Instead, they had mustered into ranks and left their home base of Mt. Othrys to penetrate deep into Olympian territory. Their progress climaxed with a furious charge up Mt. Olympus. At this point, the clashing of the armies became so intense that the mountain itself was shaken. Desperate to repel the attackers, Zeus initiated a furious counter-charge, surging forward with his lightning bolts. With this bold move, the Olympians finally gained the upper hand and routed the Titans. The vanquished gods were banished to Tartarus, with the exception of Atlas, who was sentenced to hold up the sky for eternity. Never again would they rise again from this ignominious defeat.

This thrilling tale is one of the oldest in western culture. It has been recounted down through the centuries, beginning with Hesiod, whose epic poem *Theogony* ("The birth of the gods"), was written around 730–700 B.C., and, most recently, by young adult novelist Rick Riordan. His version of the war appears in the 2008 book *The Battle of the Labyrinth*.

Of course, unlike Vietnam, Korea, Verdun, Waterloo, Leningrad, or any number of other real-world, protracted wars, the Titanomachy is the stuff of pure legend, without a trace of factuality.

Or is it?

The field of geomythology, which blends insights from geology and mythology, suggests that, in fact, there may be some truth to the tale. Geomythology sheds light on many other fables and stories as well and shows how they often contain striking pre-scientific intuitions. This book will revisit many of these tales, including well-known ones such as Odysseus and the Cyclopes, Jason and the Golden Fleece, and the fall of Troy, as well as equally rich Aboriginal and Native American legends. This chapter will provide a brief overview of how geomythology works in the case of the Titanomachy and other legends. It will also survey the history and key ideas of geomythology and offer ways this emerging discipline can enrich both the sciences and the humanities, thus helping to bridge this "two cultures" gap. This gap was first identified by chemist-novelist C.P. Snow in an influential 1959 lecture, in which he lamented the fact that scientists and humanities scholars live in two widely divergent cultures and are blissfully ignorant of each other's works.

As for Zeus and the Titans, while it is true that they never existed, the conflict between them may have been inspired by a real-life, extremely violent natural event, that is, the eruption of the volcano Thera, which occurred in or around 1628 B.C. on the Greek archipelago of Santorini. The event was truly epic: the eruption probably reached a measure of 7 on the Volcanic Explosivity Index (VEI), the volcanic equivalent of the Richter Scale, which is used to categorize earthquakes. A 7 is classified as a "super-colossal" eruption; only a handful of explosions in history have been classified as such. The largest officially recorded eruption in modern history, which occurred in 1815 when Mt. Tambora (Indonesia) blew its top, was also a 7 on the VEI. Thera released the energy of several hundred atom bombs in less than a second ("The 11" par. 25), and its blast was of the Plinian variety. That is, it resembled the notorious eruption of Italy's Mt. Vesuvius in A.D. 79, an event described by Pliny the Younger. The Thera explosion was marked by massive columns of debris and was so cataclysmic it sent hot gases through the troposphere (the first layer of earth's atmosphere) and into the next one, the stratosphere, which extends from 9 to 31 miles high. It also wreaked havoc on the small Greek island, fragmenting it into several smaller islands, and leaving a massive caldera, or cauldron-like depression, mostly submerged, where the volcano once stood.

A historian of geology, Mott Greene, argues that the main events in the Titan-Olympian war correspond closely to the phenomena of the Thera eruption. For instance, according to Hesiod, during the battle, the ground rumbled loudly, an effect that may correspond to the sounds made often by harmonic tremors, the small earthquakes that produce hums, or other sonic effects just prior to an eruption. The impression of the shaking and groaning of the sky might have been inspired by the shock waves in the air created by this particular eruption, and Zeus's charge could have been based on a combination of ignimbrites, which are rocks formed by ash cascading down a mountain (Marshak 292), and volcanic lightning (Greene 62). Unlike non-volcanic lightning, which originates during thunderstorms, volcanic lightning is created by the "electrification of ash," and "occurs in eruptive plumes" (Cimarelli et al. 4221), particularly the kind of plumes that are common in Plinian eruptions.

As geologist Stephen Marshak notes, "[n]o two eruptions are exactly alike" (289), and every active major volcano has what Greene calls an "eruptive signature": a pattern of characteristics that enables scientists to distinguish the eruption from all others (56). In the case of Thera, its principal elements parallel the Titanomachy very closely. In a sense, then, there *was* a "Titanomachy" in ancient Greece long ago, if not between deities, then between contending natural elements.

A similar example, taken from different mythology (Norse legend), is Ragnarök. The term, traditionally translated as "the twilight of the gods," refers to a time in which the Norse deities—Thor, Odin, Loki, and others—are nearing their demise. This period culminates in a kind of Armageddon, during which time the entire pantheon fights to the death in a civil war, the sun and moon are shrouded, and the world ends. Ragnarök is heralded by a time called Fimbulvetr (Old Norse for "terrible winter"), in which extreme cold sets in and winter persists unbroken for three years.

Again, such scenarios might seem purely imaginary, and indeed well-known fantasy texts like *Game of Thrones* and the Narnian Chronicles feature periods of long, continuous winter. But once more, geomythology raises the possibility that the Norse legends and their modern successors preserve a modicum of truth. For as it happens, the seasons were, in fact, seemingly disrupted during the related extreme weather events of 535–36 A.D. and 539–40 A.D. Both episodes were probably caused by massive volcanic eruptions, which spewed tons of ash into the atmosphere, and blocked the sun for months, even years, plunging the earth into volcanic winter. That trauma is recorded by contemporary historians, who noted widespread crop failure and unseasonably cold weather. The event is also indicated in tree-ring samples (Baillie) and ice-core data (Larsen et al.). In addition, it may have influenced the Norse tales, which circulated orally in pre-Christian Iceland (first settled in 874 A.D. by Norwegian explorers), and were then set down in writing in the 13th century.

Studying the ways legends and myths may contain nuggets of scientific truth is the prime activity of geomythology. The founder of this discipline, American geologist Dorothy Vitaliano (1916–2008), was a long-time faculty member at Indiana University. The idea of geomythology was sparked for her in 1961 when she read an article by seismologist A.G. Galanopoulos. He argued that the Thera blast might be linked to the fable of Atlantis. In response, Vitaliano invented the term *geomythology* in 1966 and first used it in a lecture title the following year.

Defining Terms: Geo, Myth, Mythology

To grasp the concept of geomythology, we should first note what it is *not*. Geologist Luigi Piccardi points out that the term has been used to mean "false ideas supposedly based on geological data" (vii). Presumably, notions such as the flat earth and geocentrism would fit in this category. By contrast, Piccardi and other practitioners of geomythology define it in terms of scientific truth. Its prefix, "geo-," is a variation on Gaia, or Gaea, the Greek earth goddess (*Tella*, in the Roman pantheon), and appears in other hybrid scientific terms such as geology, of course, which is the study of the earth; geography (literally, earth writing); geomatics (the storage and transmission of geographic information); geohydrology (the study of groundwater); geophysics (the physics of the earth); geobiology (the interactions of Earth and the biosphere); geochemistry (earth's chemistry, especially rocks and minerals); geoarchaeology (the study of how natural events impact human artifacts); and geomorphology (the study of earth's physical features). In addition, there are some non-scientific terms employing this prefix, such as "geocaching."

When used in geomythology, "geo" primarily refers to geological phenomena, particularly large-scale events like earthquakes and eruptions. Yet, it is worth noting that today geology, or geoscience, approaches the study of the planet as a network. In fact, this paradigm is known as the Earth System, and it includes not only the Geosphere (the rocks) and the atmosphere, but also, in the words of a widely used geology textbook, "the hydrosphere (surface and near-surface liquid water), the cryosphere (surface and near-surface ice and snow), [and] the biosphere (the great variety of living organisms)" (Marshak 43). For this reason, geomythology can be applied not only to stories about well-known occurrences like eruptions, floods, and quakes but also to events such as asteroids and comets, the formation of sinkholes, discoveries of strange animal bones, and many more.

The terms "myth" and "mythology" are harder to pin down. As Masse et al. note, "there is no universally accepted definition of the word ['myth'], nor is there a consensus view of its nature and how it should be studied" (9). As for "mythology," the *Oxford English Dictionary* notes that the term can mean both "mythical stories, or traditional beliefs collectively" (def. 3a) *or* "the study of myths" (OED 4). Yet using the same word to explain both the thing itself, as well as reflections on that thing, is potentially confusing, a bit like employing the word "sport" to denote both a game or contest, as well as the running commentary on that game. A further complication is that "virtually all traditional knowledge keepers believe myths (and legends) to be historically *true,* whereas nearly all scientists presume they are *not*" (Masse et al. 10; my emphases).

There is dizzying variety of theories on myth. For simplicity's sake, we will consider four that have been influential in the 20th century. One is the psychoanalytic method, derived from Sigmund Freud and Carl Jung, and popularized by Joseph Campbell. In it, myths function as subconscious projections that manifest archetypally within cultures. For instance, in his well-known book *The Hero with a Thousand Faces,* Campbell sees a connection between frogs and dragons, the former being a smaller version of the latter. He then analyzes fables such as The Princess and the Frog, regarding them as expressions of "that unconscious deep … wherein are hoarded all the rejected, unadmitted, unrecognized … elements of existence" (44). Another is the sociological view of myth, set forth by Emile Durkheim in works such as *The Elementary Forms of Religious Life.* He contends that myths are invented by primitive societies "to establish genealogical relations between man and the totemic animal" (105), that is, the animal (such as a bear) worshipped by a given society. Here, myth serves a ritualistic function in helping to bind societies together. In contrast to geomythology, although this approach does include animals, "Durkheim rejected the notion that myth arises out of extraordinary manifestations of nature" (Masse et al. 13).

In this sense, Durkheim's views are similar to the theory of structuralism, as seen in the work of the anthropologist Claude Lévi-Strauss. As its name indicates, it concentrates on the *structure* of myths and legends rather than their subject-matter. If myth in this view has any truth to it, that truth has to do, not with content, but with the relations of the mythic structures to one another. As literary theorist Terry Eagleton notes, structuralists might compare two myths, one about the sun and one about the moon, for example, and would claim that "the meaning of each image is wholly a matter of ... the *relation* of one to the other. The images do not have a 'substantial' meaning, only a 'relational' one" (94). Finally, we may note the historical or contextual approach. Its apparent link with history might seem to make it more congenial to geomythology. Yet, in fact, it does not consider the possible history that might have inspired a given myth, but rather the contexts, or "the impact of the social and historical environment *in which the myth is told*" (Masse et al. 13; my emphasis). For example, folklorist Lauri Honko deploys this theory when she considers whether a Finnish cosmogonic myth (one about the creation of the world) remains a myth when it is part of a ballad that is recited by young girls, as part of a ritual dance (52).

These four approaches have been updated and fleshed out by more contemporary studies. Still, for all their variety, what is striking is that "none is seemingly willing to suggest that *a real observed natural process or event* may lie at the core of myth storylines" (Masse et al. 13; my emphasis). By contrast, when she invented geomythology, Dorothy Vitaliano contended that some myths *have* served as relatively accurate, explanatory stories for natural events throughout history, particularly before the scientific method was established.

Although geomythology was new, it had ancient roots. In fact, in her 1968 article on the subject, Vitaliano harked back to antiquity, defining geomythology as "the geological application of euhemerism" (1). To unpack this definition, we can begin by observing that the term "euhemerism" derives from Euhemerus, a Greek thinker who lived in the late 4th century B.C., and who served King Cassander of Macedonia (in northeast Greece) as a mythographer, that is, as one who compiles and writes mythic stories and tales. Euhemerus was also a traveler, and one day, while visiting the island of Panchaea (probably modern-day Socotra Island, Yemen; Figure 0.1), he claims to have made a shocking discovery: on a golden stele (a monument) was posted a list of birth and death dates of various gods.

The discovery appears to have destroyed his religious faith. As a result of this experience, Euhemerus founded a rationalistic approach to myth, indeed, we might say, a demythologizing one, which sought to uncover the roots of natural events behind claims that the gods were supernatural. This approach has had a long history. Since Euhemerus's time, it has been used both to bolster and debunk Christianity. In addition, it was applied by the Icelandic mythographer Snorri Sturluson (1179–1241) to

Figure 0.1 Socotra (Soqotra) Island, Yemen. Possible site of inspiration for
   the utopian island described by Greek mythographer Euhemerus in
   his *Sacred History*.
Source: Wikimedia Commons.

explain the natural origins of figures such as Odin. The archaeologist
Heinrich Schliemann (1822–90) also applied the method in his excava-
tions of Troy. Philosopher Herbert Spencer (1820–1903) and poet Robert
Graves (1895–1985) were influenced by this approach as well.

In formulating geomythology, Vitaliano turned to euhemerism, applying it geologically as a way to uncover real natural history behind
some myths. In doing so, she differentiated between two types of geomyths: one is etiological legends, invented well after the fact "to explain
the end results of processes which were not witnessed" (10). These include legends of North American folklore, such as the exploits of Paul
Bunyan and his blue ox, Babe. For instance, the lumberjack and his ox
allegedly created both the Grand Canyon, when Bunyan dragged his ax
behind him, as well as Minnesota's 10,000 lakes, by leaving behind their
colossal footprints, which gradually filled in with water. In fact, these
areas were formed millions of years prior to any human habitation.

The charm of these stories is undeniable, but our primary concern here is with Vitaliano's second type, the euhemeristic fables. As she remarks, these tales "seek to explain certain specific myths and legends in terms of *actual geologic events that may have been witnessed* by various groups of people" (1). In other words, while modern people may regard mythology as essentially a millennia-long game of Telephone, with crucial information being lost or distorted in transmission, in fact, a number of these stories preserve traces of real information obtained first-hand. Many have to do with occurrences that would have been memorable, even traumatic, for those who experienced them. These include floods, volcanoes, and earthquakes, as well as events that, while not necessarily life-threatening, would still evoke astonishment and wonder, such as the unearthing of strange, massive bones.

Although geomythology's main value might seem to lie in the sheer pleasure of the detective work of gleaning scientific data from old sources, the method has other uses as well, a point we will develop in our conclusion. We may briefly touch on one now, which is that geomythology has what might be called an implicit "social justice" element. As historian and folklorist Adrienne Mayor demonstrates, one important chapter in the history of the discipline is the numerous discoveries and creative misunderstandings of large, fossilized animal bones in many areas of the world. For instance, the ancient Greeks appear to have routinely encountered animal remains weathering out from storms or quakes, or when they were plowing their fields. These remains, such as those belonging to woolly mammoths, were creatively misread as the skeletons of giant heroes such as Ajax, Orestes, and Achilles.

Yet these misconstruals were, at times, not far off the mark, based as they were on careful, if fanciful, observations of the skeletons. By contrast, such bones were overlooked by Aristotle and other philosophers of the time; the remains appear to have been too anomalous for "establishment" thinkers to take seriously. Aristotle, for instance, tended to label them as outliers, "monstrous" exposures that had no place in his method of seeking normal, regular specimens (Mayor, "Fossil," 217). As a result, it was often the common people, reflecting on their discoveries, who took these important first steps toward what eventually became the discipline of paleontology.

In a similar manner, geomythology has brought recognition to marginalized groups such as First Nation tribes, Aboriginals, and African slaves by showing that their narratives and observations of nature, which were often dismissed by western scientists, in fact anticipated genuine discoveries and theorizing in science. Notions of infinite time, for instance, were set forth in western thought by figures such as the farmer-turned-geologist James Hutton (1726–97), yet the Native American tribe known as the Pit River nation, or Achumawi, had an ancient creation story that suggested that the universe is 10 billion years old (Mayor, "Fossil," 150). This is an impressive conjecture, relatively close to the figure of 13.7 billion years old now held by physicists. In addition, Aboriginals may have observed first-hand a rise in sea level some 7,000 years ago (Nunn, "Ancient Aboriginal"), and recorded the observation in their myths. Furthermore, a recent paper raises an even more astonishing possibility that Aboriginals witnessed and memorialized the formation of a volcano a staggering 35,000 years ago (Barras).

Because of such narratives, some scientists are now turning to geo-myths to supplement their research, particularly when the legends deal with events from the past that pre-date written records. Geomythology adopts, as it were, a binocular vision, with one eye firmly on scientific procedure (careful observation, replication of experiments, peer review) and another on stories from outside the scientific mainstream. It does so by proceeding cautiously, separating the wheat from the chaff, the Wegeners from the Velikovskys. Both men were initially mocked for their theories, but Alfred Wegener's notion of continental drift, first published in 1912, eventually became a mainstream geological view. By contrast, in his book *Worlds in Collision* (1950), Immanuel Velikovsky argued that in or around the 15th century B.C., Venus (the planet) was ejected by Jupiter and made a near-miss of Earth while still managing to cause all sorts of catastrophes on our planet. This theory has been vigorously rejected by virtually all scientists.

Possible Objections

There are at least three potential objections to geomythology. First, it could be argued that attempts at interdisciplinarity, though well-intended, seldom work. For instance, in the case of scholars who seek to bridge the "two cultures" gap—that is, science and the humanities—geomythology might offer an attractive solution. Yet arguably, geomythology founders on one of the common obstacles to interdisciplinarity. That objection can be adapted from a withering comment by W.V. Harris, an environmental historian, who anticipates objections to his own interdisciplinary project of constructing an environmental history of the Greek and Roman world: "No historian knows enough science and no scientist knows enough history" (1). Hence, geomythologists might well be asked, can a scholar of myth or folklore bring to bear the requisite scientific background for carrying out proper analysis of fossil discoveries? By the same token, can a scientist with no training in myth, folklore, or classical or First Nation languages do justice to ancient myths? These questions are not easily answered, but the objections are not necessarily fatal to the geomythical enterprise.

For one thing, some of its main practitioners, such as Vitaliano and Mayor, are not only highly erudite; both also fit Harris's description of "ambidextrous" researchers: "outstanding individuals who have made vigorous efforts to cross the great divide" (1). Less gifted scholars can follow suit and make every effort to keep the lines of discussion open with colleagues on the other side. Mayor's habit of regularly consulting with scientific colleagues—a move often recorded in her books—ought to be one of geomythology's best practices. And non-scholarly readers can emulate the spirit of the field's rigorously hybrid approach.

Second, geomythology might also put off some readers who regard the enterprise as a form of disillusionment, conducted in the spirit of Max Weber's *Entzauberung*, usually translated as "disenchantment," set forth in his classic work *The Sociology of Religion* (1971). That is, geomythical analysis might seem merely to deconstruct wondrous tales to expose the mundane realities behind them. Of course, the very same method might attract others. In any event, the present book will argue that while geomythology often dispels one kind of awe, it replaces it with a new kind of astonishment. In doing so, it suggests that complete demythologizing, strictly speaking, may be impossible for humans and that some kind of enchantment may be an existential necessity—even for would-be demythologizers.[1]

Magic may provide a helpful example. Matt Kaplan, a paleontologist and science correspondent for *The Economist*, interviewed Teller (the mononym is his legal name), the normally silent half of the well-known magic duo Penn & Teller, on the question of whether knowing how a trick works diminishes or enhances the pleasure of it. Teller's answer was provocative:

> To any enlightened dweller of our century, knowing increases wonder. I don't just think this, I know it. If you believe, you oversimplify in the way a child might initially believe there is no complex evolution of life. That simplification in no way increases your sense of wonder. If, however, you *know* how life came to be on our planet, the wonder is immense! ("Science of the Magical" 8; italics in original)

In a similar fashion, the kind of enchantment that can result from geomythical analysis is a sense of amazement at both the workings of nature and at human ingenuity in explaining those workings. This process is particularly evident when we consider the ways various stories and tales, as it were, encode or "record" the experiences of the survivors, whether the catastrophe was an earthquake, a volcano, a tsunami, or the uncovering of the vestiges of weird, outsized fauna. Third, it may be argued that because many geomyths are rooted in an oral culture, they tend to be inaccurate, to say the least. Returning to the Telephone analogy, if this game can produce, in mere minutes, hilarious distortions of a single word or phrase, the argument goes, how much more have ancient cultures undoubtedly garbled the events they purport to describe? For instance, commenting on the gap between oral and written versions of the Bible, geophysicist Amos Nur doubtless speaks for many skeptical modern readers when he contends that the Bible is "far from a neutral history," in part because its narratives were not committed to writing until at least 700–1000 years after the original events (66). He asks, "How reliable can such an extended oral transmission be?" Nur then extends the critique to "*any* history long maintained in an oral tradition: the biases of generations of storytellers diffuse into and taint the record of events" (66; my emphasis).

Such an objection, however, relies on a host of unproven assumptions, one being that oral communication is less accurate than written transmission. The classicist Milman Parry and his successor Albert Lord challenged this view in *The Singer of Tales* (1960), their influential study of the performances of modern-day, illiterate epic bards. While these Serbo-Croatian singers often changed certain details while reciting their tales, the narrative core was set and remained so for years. Matt Kaplan notes that Parry originally recorded these recitals in 1934, and when Lord returned to the area over 15 years later, in 1950, the stories had not been altered ("Science of the Magical" 89). Thus, *The Singer of Tales* undermined the modern presumption that "a given [oral] text undergoes change from one singing to another" (Lord 99). In fact, the bards appeared to view a song as "a flexible plan of themes" (Lord 99), similar to the way jazz musicians regard their own compositions.

In addition, as the scholars Elizabeth and Paul Barber contend, oral stories that recorded particularly tumultuous, wrenching events—precisely the kind that appears to have inspired many geomyths—seem to have been encoded, in a sense, to permit ease of transfer, as well as accuracy, down through time. They note that "before writing, myths had to serve as transmission systems for information deemed important." However, modern readers "have lost track of how to decode the information often densely compressed into these stories" (2). As a result, today, we tend to hear the myths as little more than outlandish fables.

To address this issue, the Barbers analyze a powerful First Nation myth from the Klamath tribe in Oregon. It is one of the most commonly cited legends in geomythical research and involves a battle between the gods associated with two mountains, Mt. Mazama and Mt. Shasta. One deity, the "Chief of the Below World," falls in love with a lovely young woman who is the daughter of a local chieftain, but when he expresses his feelings to her, she spurns him. To avenge his wounded pride he stands atop Mt. Mazama and begins to wreak vengeance on her village. At the same time, the "Chief of the Above World" descends from the sky and alights on Mt. Shasta.

The two chiefs then clash in an exchange of thunder, burning rain, and boulders. Meanwhile, the villagers seek refuge from the fiery barrage in Klamath Lake while their two medicine men confer with one another on how to appease the warring gods. The men agree to light torches and ascend Mt. Mazama, and once they summit it, they pause at the top and gaze in. After hesitating for a moment, the men lift their torches, then leap into the crater as self-sacrifices (6–7). When the Chief of the Above World witnesses this stunning act, he drives the Below World chief into Mazama for good, then brings the entire mountain down on the malcontent. By morning, all that is left is a caldera that fills with rain, eventually becoming Crater Lake.

Today, geologists have pieced together the area's history, and astonishingly, their findings align with the Klamath legend: Crater Lake is indeed the result of a caldera formed about 7,000 years ago. Perhaps most startling here is the antiquity of the story. That is, long before researchers reached their conclusions about the caldera, the essential narrative was memorialized and preserved in the Klamath culture. It would seem, then, that harrowing natural events often impress themselves on the mind, or in the case of a myth, within an entire culture's collective memory. This process is reinforced when the myth appears to have been intended as a cautionary tale, as is the case with the Crater Lake story. Indeed, probably as a result of the legend, the Klamath people avoided this body of water for generations, to the consternation of white explorers who wanted to learn more about the lake (Barber and Barber 7).

In their words, Patrick Nunn suggests that the Klamath believed that "terrible things happened [at Crater Lake], involving beings more powerful than us mortals, beings whom we suspect still dwell there." For this reason, Nunn continues, "[i]t is likely that the memory of Mt. Mazama was kept alive for such an extraordinarily long time because it was considered to contain … practical advice relating to the survival of the Klamath people" ("Recalling"). Such may be the case with a number of geomyths: the events they record were so shattering that story and myth alone were up to the task of somehow explaining them. In this light, links between geomythology and the literary/cultural field known as trauma theory might be profitably explored in future studies.[2]

Is Geomythology a Science?

The origins of modern science remain contested, yet many historians agree that it commenced with the so-called Scientific Revolution, generally dated as beginning in 1543 with the publication (on his deathbed) of Copernicus's *De Revolutionibus Orbium Coelestium*, which advances the theory of heliocentrism (that is, with the sun rather than the earth at the center). This book inaugurated a period in which thinkers such as Francis Bacon, Galileo, Kepler, Copernicus, and others initiated an empirical, systematic study of nature and threw off the stifling influences of figures such as Aristotle, whose thinking was mainly deductive, top-down, and non-experimental. Yet even if we accept that *De Revolutionibus* ignited the scientific enterprise, it is also true that prior to 1543, oral cultures also carefully observed nature and made informed guesses about its workings.

For example, the griffin, a legendary hybrid creature with an eagle's head and lion's body, has engaged writers from Aeschylus to J.K. Rowling. The animal is reputed to be a fierce guardian of gold treasure and is clearly fanciful. Yet historian/folklorist Adrienne Mayor makes a strong case that in antiquity, artistic and literary depictions of the griffin may have been influenced by real-life encounters between travelers in central Asia and the skeletons of the dinosaur *Protoceratops* found in the Gobi Desert. She also shows how the griffin, with its quadruped morphology, quickness, and warm-bloodedness, presages the Dinosaur Renaissance, which began in the late 1960s and sought to leave behind outdated views of dinosaurs as sluggish and cold-blooded ("First," 15–53).

Is it possible, then, to regard geomythology as a science, having the same status as other hybrids such as geochemistry or geohydrology? At this point, the answer is no. For one thing, the old stories are often murky, anonymous, and extant in varying, sometimes contradictory, versions. For another, it is an unresolved, and probably unresolvable, chicken-or-egg question as to whether myths were inspired by the discovery and misidentification of physical evidence, or whether the stories came first and were then "confirmed" by the evidence, creatively misconstrued. Indeed, it is entirely possible that the geomyths discussed in this book are purely fanciful, the result of imagination, nothing more. That said, there are also contraindications, particularly when we focus on geomyths that appear to be closely linked to physical remnants and/or eyewitness accounts.

In any case, science has not embraced geomythology, though various inroads by the emerging field may be noted. Not only was its founder Dorothy Vitaliano, as noted, a geologist, the 32nd (2004) International Geological Conference offered a session on "Myth and Geology," and that meeting resulted in a 2007 collection of peer-reviewed papers (Piccardi & Masse). A recent search for "geomythology" on the *Science Direct* website brought up 25 peer-reviewed scientific articles, and a similar quest on *Google Scholar* yielded approximately 630 results. Then again, unlike the phrases "geomorphology" and "geohydrology," the term "geomythology" has not made it into the *Oxford English Dictionary*, nor is the word listed in *The Oxford Dictionary of Geology and Earth Sciences* (2013), the *McGraw-Hill Dictionary of Geology and Mineralogy* (2003), or Marshak's *Earth: Portrait of a Planet* (2015), a popular earth sciences textbook. Even so, the *Encyclopedia of Geology* (2005) features an article on the subject by Mayor.

That article demonstrates that while geomythology was officially inaugurated in the 1960s, in a sense, its methods were anticipated centuries prior and often yielded striking, proto-scientific intuitions. One is the fact that, as noted, Euhermerus's method of analysis anticipates modern, rationalistic approaches to myth. His protégé Palaephatus, for instance, deployed a proto-geomythic stance in his analysis of the origins of Thebes, a Greek city. According to the story, the hero Cadmus was sent by the Delphic oracle to a certain uninhabited spot. Upon arrival, Cadmus sent two of his companions to fetch water from a spring. Unfortunately, a water-dragon slew them, so Cadmus avenged them by killing the beast. Athena then told Cadmus to sow the dragon's teeth in the ground, and when he did so, an army of fierce soldiers sprung up. These were the Spartans—*spartoi* means "sown"—who helped him establish a settlement. (The city-state of Sparta is named not for *spartoi*, but for its founding mythical queen.)

As Mayor points out, Palaephatus recognized that the teeth of the "dragon" may, in fact, have been fossilized elephant molars ("Geomythology" 1). This conjecture could well have been based on the discovery of mastodon teeth, which are pointed, in contrast to the flat surfaces of mammoth molars. We may also note that the size and sharpness of the teeth naturally could have suggested a kind of ferocity, evident both in the harvested Spartans, who were known for their valor in battle, and in the animal from whose savage jaws the teeth putatively dropped. (Up until the 18th century, mastodons were believed to be carnivorous by Thomas Jefferson and others, in part because of the striking visual appearance of their dentition.)

Other classical texts, Mayor argues, also have geomythical facets. Plato's two accounts of Atlantis "correctly described large-scale changes in prehistoric land masses and coastlines in the Aegean" (1 2). And Ovid's *Metamorphoses* demonstrates an accurate grasp of basic geomorphology as well as petrifaction. Strabo, an ancient Greek geographer, even seemed to anticipate geomythical reasoning when he notes that some myths express "physical notions ... by adding mythical elements." We may also bring the poet Virgil into the discussion here, since in *The Aeneid*, Book III, he writes, "The tale goes that the body of Enceladus [a mythical giant], / Half consumed by thunderbolt, lies prone under that weight, prodigious Aetna piled / Above him ..." (767–70). The poet's qualifier "The tale goes" implies some doubt regarding the narrative's literal truth.

Turning from the ancients to the moderns, one notable figure for geomythology is the polymath Robert Hooke (1635–1703), an inventor, physicist, astronomer, and architect. After the fire of 1666, he submitted plans for rebuilding St. Paul's Cathedral and became the London city surveyor. Hooke was the intellectual peer of Isaac Newton, with whom he feuded. Historian of science Allan Chapman calls him "England's Leonardo." Mayor points out that in his *Lectures and Discourses of Earthquakes and Subterranean Eruptions*, delivered in 1667–68, Hooke grappled with the claim that fossils are the remains of organic creatures, rather than inorganic substances that merely appear as if they were once alive. One difficulty raised by the organic view is the question of why marine fossils are buried so far from present-day seas. That is, if they are the vestiges of once-living creatures, they should, in theory, be found only near the oceans. Hooke's answer relied on the action of earthquakes and volcanoes, both to raise up the seafloor and create mountains, and to form islands. He cited as evidence the ancients, such as Plato's accounts of Atlantis and the Titan-Olympian war, and argued, geomythically, that these events are oblique descriptions of such events ("Geomythology" 2).

Another influential scientist who invoked geomyths is the father of paleontology, Georges Cuvier (1769–1832). In formulating his theory of global species extinction, Cuvier assembled a list of First Nation myths along with Greek tales to "demonstrate the worldwide distribution and long-standing observations of the fossilized remains of immense creatures." He was also the first scientist to grasp that these remains belonged to extinct elephants (2). In a similar fashion, Edward B. Tylor (1832–1917), the founder of cultural anthropology, studied traditional myths, referring to them as "myths of observation," that is, careful attempts to explain mysterious things discovered in nature (Mayor, "Geomythology" 2).

When considering 20th- and 21st century researchers who have used geomythical logic, several stand out. In addition to Vitaliano is the seismologist A.G. Galanopoulos, who was already mentioned. He was one of the first to apply this approach to the Atlantis myth in his 1969 book *Atlantis: The Truth Behind the Legend*. Likewise, geologist Jörg Keller deployed geomythology to date within 50 years the eruption of a volcano on the island of Lipari, west of the toe of Italy's "boot" (Vitaliano 95). Contemporary figures in the field include Adrienne Mayor, geographer Patrick Nunn, and astronomer Duane Hamacher. The latter two have published research focusing on the geomythical potential of Aboriginal narratives.

In sum, while geomythology is not regarded as a science, it has proven to be an invaluable ally to researchers over the centuries and has helped to confirm a number of scientific discoveries. Chapter 4 will take up the science/geomythology question again and ask whether and how geomythology might someday not merely confirm but stimulate scientific research.

Geomythology and the Humanities

Geomythology can enrich the humanities in theories such as trauma studies, as noted, as well as discourses of enchantment. Furthermore, it overlaps significantly with ecocriticism, a discipline that seeks to examine, in the words of an influential practitioner, "the relationship between literature and the physical environment" (Glotfelty xviii). One study, for instance, approaches the Old English poem *Beowulf* in terms of geomythology and ecocriticism (Burbery, "Fossil"). Given that a primary goal of ecocriticism is the replacement of, or balancing of, anthropocentric views with ecocentric ones, geomythology is of value. For two of geomythology's main tasks, as we have argued, is understanding how humans have creatively projected human desires and images onto nature, and comprehending the underlying natural events that inspired such projections. In a sense, when we discover the event that inspired a myth, it is as if nature is "writing back," undercutting the confidence of storytellers that, say, certain gigantic bones surely must have belonged to a human being rather than to an animal.

Geomythology may, in addition, buoy environmental justice and indigenous studies as well as related fields such as post-colonialism, by recovering little-known narratives and perspectives from marginalized peoples and showing how their observations often provide salient proto-scientific intimations. One notable example is the slaves of Stono Plantation (North Carolina), who in or around 1725 correctly identified some large, recently unearthed molars as belonging to an elephantine species, rather than, as white observers surmised, to a human giant who perished in Noah's Flood. Many of these slaves were born and raised in Angola or the Congo and were thus presumably familiar with elephant bones (Mayor, "Slaves First"). In addition, geomythology has brought to light forgotten chapters in the history of science, such as the fact that often, the guides for white, western paleontologists in the fossil fields of the United States were members of First Nation tribes who had already observed exposed bones, well before the explorers came on the scene (Mayor, "Fossil" xxv).

One notable contribution to indigenous studies is the book *Do Glaciers Listen?: Local Knowledge, Colonial Encounters, and Social Imagination* (2014), in which anthropologist Julie Cruikshank contrasts European and native views of glaciers in the Alaskan Panhandle during the last stages of the Little Ice Age (A.D. 1550–1850). In their myths, the indigenes tended to see glaciers as alive: they named them, gendered them, and prohibited certain behavior they felt might anger the ice-masses, such as lighting cooking fires on their surfaces.

Both European and native groups became explorers when, near the end of the period, the glaciers started to melt. Newly exposed land opened up, and westerners and First Nation peoples alike began to study these areas. Cruikshank compares and contrasts the oral traditions spoken by the elders (all women) with the notebooks of the explorers. She describes her methods as follows: "I rely on both written and oral accounts, trying to privilege neither but rather to see how both kinds of accounts illuminate past worlds and shed light on present interpretations" ("Practices"). Perhaps surprisingly, the accounts overlap to a great extent. Hence, Cruikshank's work helps to affirm the geomythical insight that pre-scientific local knowledge can play a role in the production of scientific knowledge. We will see how this insight is affirmed in subsequent chapters, especially in terms of Chinese dragon stories and narratives about Pele, the Hawaiian volcanic deity.

Finally, geomythology can help to resolve interpretive questions and issues in the humanities. For instance, as I will show in Chapter 1, there is a passage in Virgil's *Aeneid* in which the corpse of the slain king of Troy is said to be headless and lying on a beach. This is a strange description, since the description of Priam's death earlier in the poem makes no mention of his being decapitated, nor does he perish outside the city walls, but rather, within the citadel of Troy. Geomythology can shed light on this difficult passage. In a similar manner, the ancient Greek historian Herodotus (484-425 B.C.) has long been accused of exaggerating or embellishing his material. Indeed, he is sometimes referred to as the "Father of Lies." Yet I believe that geomythology can help to exonerate him, somewhat, as I will demonstrate in Chapter 3.

To initiate our study of geomythology, we will begin broadly, then narrow our focus. The first two chapters will look at tales that seem nearly universal, including stories of dragons, giants, volcanoes, floods, earthquakes, and tsunamis. It will also consider pre-scientific insights embedded in these fables. Chapter 3 concentrates on legends linked to specific regions or areas of the world. These feature, among other things, griffins, gold-mining ants, meteors, people-eating birds, and "killer" lakes. Again, we will engage the ways scientists have examined these phenomena. Chapter 4 brings us full circle by returning to the kind of theoretical questions engaged in Chapter 1, and considering how geomythology might develop in the future.

Notes

1 For instance, in his 2017 book *The Myth of Disenchantment: Magic, Modernity, and the Birth of the Human Sciences*, historian Jason Josephson-Storm argues that Weber, Rudolph Carnap, Max Müller, Marie Curie, and other figures of the early 20th century were heavily involved in the spiritualist and occultist milieu. Josephson-Storm's book has generally garnered positive reviews, though Doug Sikemma takes him to task on a number of points, including the fact that, contrary to Josephson-Storm, Curie attended a séance not as a participant but in order to debunk the spiritualist's claims (101).
2 Tom Shippey's notion of "traumatised authors" (xvii) might be useful in this regard. In his study of Tolkien, *The Road to Middle-earth*, Shippey argues that modern fantasy writers such as Tolkien, C.S. Lewis, Kurt Vonnegut, George Orwell, and others were so emotionally—and often physically—devastated by the horrors of the 20th century, including the major wars, that they turned to the fantasy genre in composing *Lord of the Rings*, *The Chronicles of Narnia*, *Slaughter-House Five*, and *1984*, respectively, to come to grips with what they had experienced on the battlefield.

1   Universal Geomyths (Part I)

Dragons

One way to approach geomythology is to start with legends that are common to many cultures, such as dragon stories, giant fables, and volcano myths. These narratives are so pervasive as to be nearly universal, even archetypal. Again, we must admit the possibility that they sprang solely from the imaginations of storytellers down through the ages. Even so, there may yet be geological or paleontological events that could have influenced their creation. We begin with dragons, perhaps the most widely known of all legendary creatures. Whether it be the formidable fire-breathers of *Game of Thrones*; or medieval legends, as in St. George and the dragon; or Smaug, from *The Hobbit*; or Lewis Carroll's draconic "Jabberwocky"; or dragon bones in Chinese medicine; or encounters of First Nation tribes with dinosaur eggs and bones, dragon stories abound throughout the world.

However, their very ubiquity presents a considerable obstacle, which is finding fresh ways to discuss creatures whose legends saturate the western mind. Fortunately, geomythical approaches have been innovative in this area. We will consider three topics in the following order: Chinese dragon lore, dragon teeth and skulls, and draconic landscapes. One striking fact for western readers is that in Chinese, historically, the phrase "dragon" applies to *all* fossil bones, not just those that might evoke a traditionally draconic appearance (Mayor, "Fossil" 21). Mayor notes that a key source for knowledge of "dragon bones" is the *I Ching* ("Book of Changes"), an ancient divination text. In the third "Qian" section, there are references to dragons "appearing in the field" ("Chinese"), and these manifestations are regarded as good omens since "dragon" bones were often used for folk remedies in China. Indeed, bone-based medicine became popular enough that at one point, in north China, a bone works was operative. It functioned

Figure 1.1 Chinese flag featuring an antlered dragon. Wikimedia Commons.

like a mine, in which workers "extracted heavy, calcified bones with pulleys and sifted sediments in baskets" (Mayor, "Fossil" 39). Among its findings were remains of what we now recognize as deer and horses. As Mayor notes, "certain features of the traditional Chinese dragon, such as the distinctive antlers resembling those of fossil deer," may be based on the remains of Pliocene and Pleistocene mammals (39) (Figure 1.1). Such folk traditions also reinforce Julie Cruikshank's point that local knowledge can assist scientists in their research, for in their study of dinosaur footprints in China, Xing et al. note that "[r]ecently, Chinese paleontologists have discovered heretofore un-known dinosaur deposits by enlisting the help of farmers familiar with locations of dragon bones" (18).

Regarding other non-western stories of dragons, there are Indian tales of such creatures, who were alleged to live in the Siwalik Hills, at the foot of the Himalayas. Not surprisingly, this area contains rich deposits of Pleistocene remains. Among these are tusks, bones, and jaws of the four-horned giraffes, camels, smilodons, giant turtles, and prehistoric elephants known as *proboscideans*. Philostratus the Athenian (A.D. 170–250) wrote a biography of the sage and philoso-pher Apollonius of Tyana (3 B.C. - A.D. 97), who traveled to India to meet with the intellectuals there. Among other things, Apollonius hoped to glimpse the animals who were said to live under the surface of the Himalayas and who sported crests and jewels in their skulls (Mayor, "First" 129–30). The fact that they supposedly resided in the earth points to their fossil origins. According to Philostratus, the skulls of these dragons were shown in the city of Paraka, which may correspond to the modern city of Peshawar. These skulls plausibly belonged, in fact, to extinct giraffes such as Sivatheriums, or elephants of the region. Somewhat reminiscent of Chinese dragons, the *Giraffokeryx* had four horns and thus probably looked quite draconic, and *Sivartherium Giganteum*–whose first name, based on the god Shiva, provides a small example of mythology's impact on science–was quite large and possessed two colossal antlers. As for the jewels, Mayor speculates that this detail "alludes to the crystals that can form on mineralized bones," and notes that "large, glittering calcite crystals and tubular selenite crystals are common in the Siwalik fossils" ("The First" 133).

Turning to the lore of Grecian dragon narratives, we briefly noted earlier that the story of Cadmus, dragon-slayer, and founder of Thebes, was analyzed in a proto-geomythical manner by Palaephatus. In his 4th century (B.C.) treatise *On Unbelievable Tales*, Palaephatus recounts the legend, then offers a rational explanation, which is that Cadmus slew, not a dragon, but a king named Draco (Latin for "dragon"), who owned some elephant teeth. The teeth were housed, Palaephatus alleges, in a temple but were pilfered by Cadmus's allies, who subsequently sold them to raise armies (Mayor, "The First," 222). Moreover, it is possible that if actual pachyderm teeth were involved, they might well have belonged to a mastodon. As mentioned above, unlike woolly mammoths, whose flat teeth resemble the tread of a running shoe, mastodons' were jagged. The latter seems more likely to have conjured tales of a meat-eating beast (Figure 1.2).

Thebes is not the only city founded on a legendary dragon-killing. Another is Klagenfurt, in southern Austria, situated on Lake Wörthersee. Its builders were harassed by a lindworm, a dragon (generally wingless) that is common in Nordic and Germanic lore. Eventually, two valiant men killed it, thereby allowing construction to proceed. Although this tale is fanciful, it is interesting to note that "Klagenfurt" means "ford of lament" or "ford of complaint," and could indicate that there was a genuine disturbance connected with the waters adjoining the town. Perhaps a large eel was glimpsed during a time of crisis in the area, then alchemized into the dragon fable. In any case, a monument in the town square features two statues, one of the lindworm (winged, in this case), the other of Hercules. The works

(a)

(b)

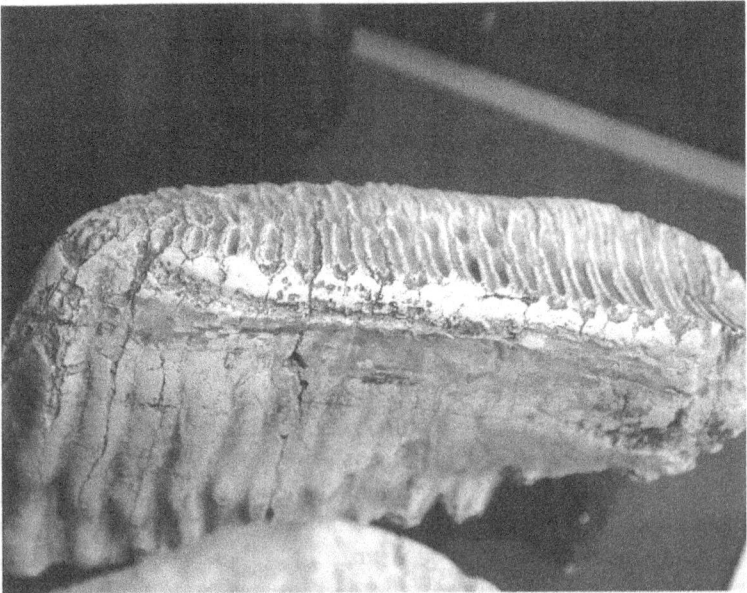

Figure 1.2 (a) Mastodon teeth. (b) Mammoth teeth. Wikimedia Commons. Photo of 1.2 (b) by Rama.

Figure 1.3 Lindworm and Hercules statues, Klagenfurt, Austria. Johann Jeritz, 2020. Wikimedia Commons.

reinforce each other thematically since Hercules's second labor was to dispatch the Hydra, who, as its name indicates, was associated with water (Figure 1.3).

Yet, the lindworm statue was not merely symbolic or fanciful for the sculptors. We know this because a supposed dragon skull was uncovered in an Austrian quarry in 1335 and was used as a model for the head of the Klagenfurt statue, which was constructed in 1590. In reality, the skull probably came from a woolly rhino. Like the more famous woolly mammoths, these rhinos lived during the Pleistocene, which was one of Earth's ice ages. Seas were lower in the Pleistocene because more water was frozen in the polar caps. Worldwide temperatures were also lower, as evidenced by the greater prevalence of glaciers. Indeed, it is estimated that about 30% of the earth was covered with ice during this period, as opposed to 10% today. As a consequence, as animals such as rhinos and pachyderms evolved, they grew fur to cope.

Daniel Ogden, a classics scholar, provides another inventive approach to dragon study, coining the phrase "dragonscapes" to examine legendary "evidence" of their actions in ancient topography. In his words, he surveys "the [supposed] signs ... that the great dragons had left on the land – a seemingly burned quality in the rock, or a bloody one, a hill constricted into shape by coils, a meandering riverbed carved out by a serpentine slither, [or] a former cave-home" (15). Ogden does so in relation to well-known monsters including Typhon, who opposed Zeus in the Gigantomachy, the war that followed the Titanomachy; the Python, or Delphic dragon; the Chimera, which was at least partly draconic; and the dragonish sea monster Cetus.

Typhon's inclusion in Ogden's list might seem problematic, given that most accounts portray Typhon, not as a dragon, but as a composite of human, animal, and serpentine features. Hesiod depicts him as such, as do Nonnus and Apollodorus (165). Yet Ogden points out that a Greek vase, circa 570–50 B.C., has recently come to light; it shows beyond question that "Typhon was fundamentally a *drakon*." It depicts "a striding, bearded Zeus, identified by his lightning-bolt, grasping a great serpent by the neck as he prepares to dash the thunderbolt down upon it; this pure serpent, *unhybridised with any other creature,* can only be Typhon himself, given that he is the only known opponent of Zeus with any serpentine element" (166; my emphasis).

There is a relatively high number of Typhonic signs throughout the Mediterranean, based on his brawl with Zeus. They include the claim that after their fight, Zeus buried the monster under the region between Vesuvius and the Phlegraean Fields, an area in central Italy that smokes and fumes to this day from volcanic activity (166). Additionally, the so-called Katakekaumene ("Burnt Land"), situated in western Turkey, is characterized by black rocks "that even now give the impression of burning" (166). According to the ancient geographer Strabo (*Geographica*), Zeus and Typhon dueled to the death here, as Zeus scored the landscape with his thunderbolts. Another is Mt. Haemus (Haimos), located in the Balkan Peninsula and supposedly named for the blood (*haima*) that spurted forth from the dragon when the All-Father crushed him under Mt. Aetna. Moreover, the winding Orontes River, whose mouth is in western Turkey, was alleged to have been created inadvertently by Typhon when he "squirmed across the surface of the earth … to evade Zeus's thunderbolts" (166). In fact, in *Geographica* 16.2, Strabo alleges that "Typhon" was the Orontes's original name. Finally, there is the Corycian Cave in Cilicia (southern Turkey), reputed to be Typhon's lair. It is actually a massive sinkhole, 128 meters (420 feet) deep, but its opening is relatively small, giving it a cave-like appearance. While we cannot call any of these fables geomythical, given their post hoc orientation, they do manifest an awareness of each location's geomorphology.

Giants and Fossilized Bones

Giant fables, like draconic ones, are also widespread. Not only do giants appear in Greek stories; some, like the Cyclopes, feature both in Greek texts (Hesiod's *Theogony*, Homer's *Odyssey*) and Roman ones (Virgil's *Aeneid*). The first great work of English literature, *Beowulf*, depicts the hero going up against Grendel and his mother, both of whom are huge, humanoid fiends. In English folklore, the hero Jack climbs a beanstalk and makes his way into the castle of a giant, who calls out, ominously and famously, "fee-fi-foe-fum / I smell the blood of an Englishman," when he senses Jack's presence. Bilbo Baggins and his nephew Frodo Baggins encounter massive trolls in *The Hobbit* and *The Lord of the Rings*, respectively, and giants appear in George R.R. Martin's *Game of Thrones*. They are present as well in non-western stories like those of the Daityas in Hindu mythology and in fables of the Si-Te-Cah, the cannibalistic, red-haired tribe of giants of Paiute legends.

Of course, there have been very large human beings throughout history, and they alone could have inspired giant fables. However, some mythic titans may have sprung from the misrecognition of fossilized animal bones, especially mastodon and mammoth remains. Why this is so requires some explanation. We have touched on the appearances of mammoth and mastodon teeth, yet both species also possessed a morphology that looked startlingly human, especially in terms of their femurs (thighbones), scapulae (shoulder blades), and ribcages. All of these bones can seem like super-sized versions of human ones, especially when viewed in isolation.

It might seem that the presence of tusks alongside these other remains in mammoth graveyards would be a dead giveaway, so to speak, that any other bones near the tusks probably did not belong to humans. However, the ancients did not always regard tusks as related to the rest of the skeletons. In fact, they seem to have correctly recognized, often, that tusks were made of ivory, while also believing, inaccurately if creatively, that these remains sprang from the ground like minerals, not from animals (Burbery, "Geomythology" 86). We also know that while mammoth femurs and scapulae tended to be very durable and often survived for millennia, the skulls of such creatures were relatively fragile and frequently crumbled easily. Hence, it would not be uncommon to find femurs, scapulae, and ribs without any telltale skulls near them.

Moreover, a significant number of mammoth and mastodon remains are buried in seismically active regions like Greece and Italy, and hence, to this day, they often appear after earthquakes or storms. As geophysicist Amos Nur points out, "the Aegean region is a hot-bed of seismic activity." He sums up the tectonics of this area, movements that have been going on for millions of years: "The Arabian [tectonic] plate is moving north [about 15–20 mm per year] relative to the African plate ... the Anatolian plate is moving west, and the European plate is moving southeast" (230; see Figure 1.4). The result is strong, frequent quakes.

As for bones becoming visible after such events, both ancient and contemporary examples are not difficult to find. The Simi Valley (CA)

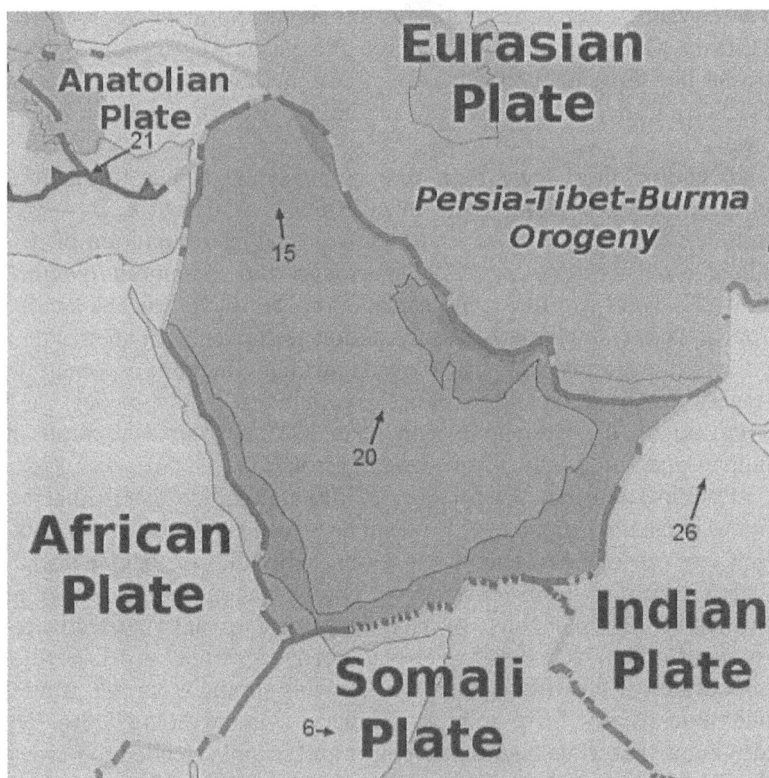

Figure 1.4 The Arabian Plate (center), which underlies Saudi Arabia. The arrows indicate the direction of the movements of this plate, along with the African, Anatolian, Eurasian, Indian, and Somali Plates. The numbers represent the millimeters each plate covers annually. Alataristarion, 2015. Wikimedia Commons.

earthquakes of 2019 exposed at least one fossil, possibly from a whale or hippo ("California"). Furthermore, the New Madrid (Missouri) earthquakes of 1811–12 created, among other things, "sand blows," or "cratered mounds of sand," and one such "blow ... spit out the fossilized skull of an extinct musk ox" Boer and Sanders ("Earthquakes" 121). In antiquity, the Neades were said to be colossal beasts who lived on the Greek island of Samos, according to the mythographer Euagon of Samos, writing in the 5th century B.C. At times, the Neades roared so loudly the earth would open up and swallow them (Mayor, "Fossil" 57). Samos has strong quakes today as well, which are often accompanied by noises, along with freshly exposed bones. The Neades legend seems to reflect such manifestations.

What is more, the bones that surface are often disarticulated and jumbled, given the potency of these quakes, which in this region tend to be tectonic events. These are caused by the shifting of plates and are usually deeper than volcanic tremors. We also know that in antiquity, neither mammoths nor mastodons were recognized as species that were distinct from elephants, as well as extinct. In fact, the very concept of extinction was not established in western science until Cuvier proposed it in the 1800s. Finally, we recognize that humans are highly prone to seeing apparently humanoid forms in nature—in cloud formations, in the Man in the Moon, in the "face" on Mars, and so on. Summing up, then, it would seem that at least some of the giants in myth were based on the misidentification of animal bones as the remnants of large persons. And if the remnants were discovered near sites such as Troy, it also seems plausible that they were identified by the ancients as belonging to fallen heroes from the epic, such as King Priam, Achilles, or Ajax (Burbery, "Geomythology" 85) (Figure 1.5a and b).

Admittedly, we have no proof of these identifications, no record of an author explicitly stating that he or she made such a link. Hence, geomythology remains more art than science. Even so, connections are conceivable, as many mythical giants are associated with the same regions where mammoth and mastodon bone deposits are located. Indeed, one of the most compelling pieces of evidence in Adrienne Mayor's book on ancient fossil-hunters is a map that superimposes the sites of modern discoveries of animal bones onto areas where "monsters" were unearthed long ago ("The First" 114). In most cases, the two locales match up.

These potential connections may help explain the origins of perhaps the most iconic race of giants, the Cyclopes. As we saw earlier, in *Theogony,* they help Zeus defeat the Titans, yet in Homer and Virgil, the Cyclopes are portrayed as hairy, monocular, cannibalistic ogres.

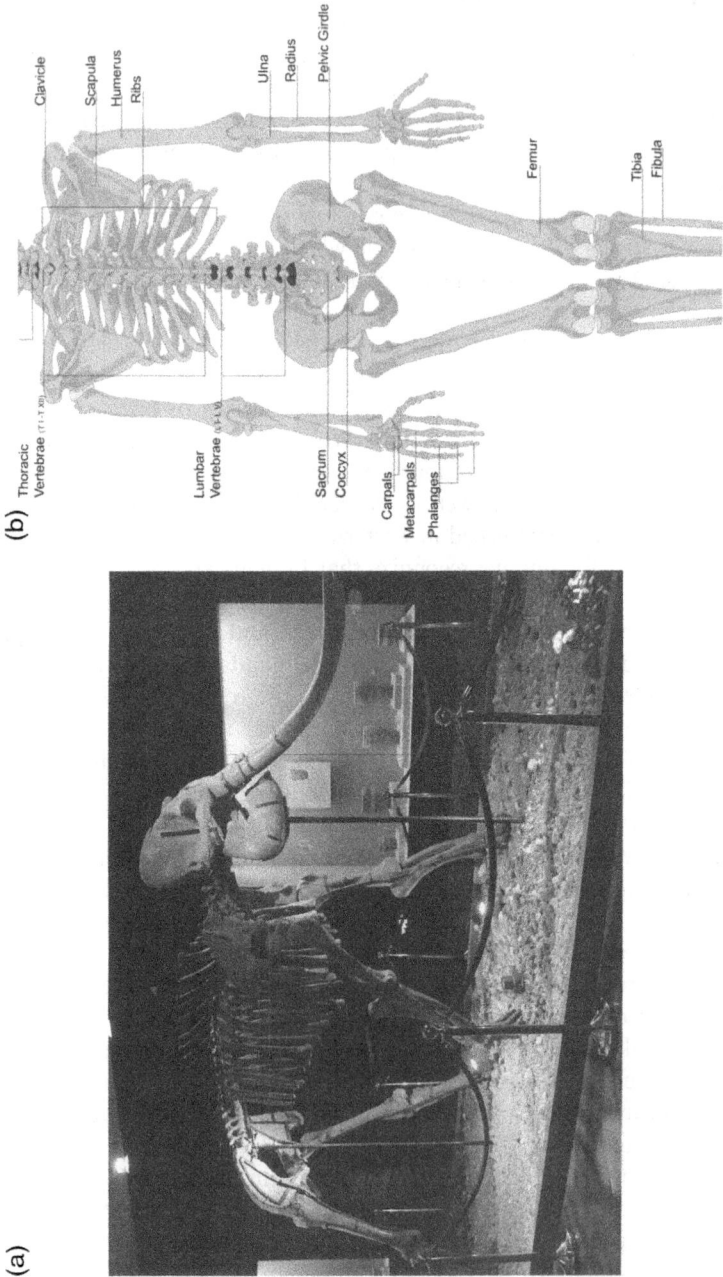

Figure 1.5 (a) Mastodon skeleton. Photo by Gary Todd, 2014. (b) Human female skeleton, back view. Note the similarities of the ribcages, femurs, and shoulder-blades.

The Odyssey contains the most famous Cyclopean narrative, in which Odysseus and his crew are trapped in the cave of Polyphemus, a Cyclops who snatches up two men at a time, bashes their heads on rocks, then gorges himself on them. He does so again the next day as the remaining men watch helplessly. Eventually, the prisoners get the monster drunk on some heady wine they happened to have smuggled into the cave. The giant then falls asleep, at which point they stab his enormous eye with a sharpened, fire-heated stake made from an olive tree. Polyphemus roars with outrage but of course can no longer see the men to crush them. Soon after, they escape his lair by strapping themselves to the undersides of the ogre's sheep.

A host of explanations for this creature has been offered over the last two centuries. Nature-based accounts include attempts to read the Cyclops as inspired by, respectively, the moon; the glowing of Mt. Etna's night fires; the eye of a storm; and a gorilla (Glenn 142, 143). In Glenn's view, such interpretations are "far-fetched and unconvincing, since none of them successfully bridges the huge gap between the sun (moon, etc.) and the cannibal-giant that we find in Homer." He castigates this approach as Procrustean, "starting from the preconception that a particular phenomenon in nature holds the key to myths," then forcing the evidence to conform (142). Other scholars, like Kirk, have abandoned the search for these tales' origins (Glenn 148). More recently, D'Huy has noted that "the problem of the physical, geographical origin of this story ... seems unsolvable" (48).

Even so, geomythical analysis may shed some light here. To understand how, one issue must be cleared up first. Regarding the ogre's monocular condition, there have been medical cases of people being born with only one eye situated in the middle of their heads. Aptly, the disorder is known as *cyclopism*. An infant girl born in India in 2011 was afflicted with it and lived just 24 hours (Hartzman). Given that cyclopism is a severe birth defect, it is hard to imagine anyone who has it surviving even briefly, let alone to adulthood. Furthermore, as medical researcher Edward Nelson argues, genuine cyclopism results in a human with the mouth being *over*, rather than under, the eye—which is not the case in Homer or in Virgil.[1]

In Homer, Odysseus and his men register the enormity of Polyphemus, both indirectly, by the huge pines and boulders he uses to wall up his cave, and directly, when they see his "monstrous hulk" (IX. 289) and stare, agog, as he grabs two of Odysseus's seasoned warriors and feasts on them. In a similar fashion, Virgil's Cyclops narrative, spoken briefly by the character Achaemenides, explicitly emphasizes the giant's size. When Aeneas and his men first see the colossus, they are repelled by his "[v]ast, mind-sickening, lumpish" form (III. 872), and they watch him washing out his "gouged eye-pit" (878). This section presumably would be an appropriate place for Virgil to mention, in addition, a mouth situated above the eye, but he does not, further weakening the notion that these literary representations could have been based on any unfortunate human being suffering from cyclopism.

One intriguing, proto-geomythical explanation was offered by Austrian paleontologist Othenio Abel in 1914. He suggested that the monsters were evoked by mistaken interpretations of dwarf elephant skulls. Such remains were misconstrued by the ancients as belonging not to a type of pachyderm, but rather, to a creature with one eye socket in the center of its head—ergo, to a Cyclops (Mayor, "First" 7). Furthermore, these elephants lived and died in caves, and their remains, like their mammoth and mastodon cousins', look human. As such, when these remnants were found by ancient peoples, they could have suggested that the Cyclopes were not only single-eyed but also cannibalistic (36).

There is a certain plausibility to Abel's theory. To see why, some background is in order. The dwarf elephant's name may sound oxymoronic, yet it stems from the fact that even normally massive creatures like elephants can become stunted over several generations when isolated on islands. As such, they are cut off from the normal range of nutriments and space non-islanded species enjoy and thus fail to flourish. Moreover, dwarf elephants were common in the Pleistocene in what is now the island of Sicily, just southwest of the Italian mainland. The Sicily-Cyclopes link is mentioned at least twice in classical sources: in Virgil's episode, already touched on, and by the normally sober-minded Greek historian Thucydides. In his *History of the Peloponnesian War* (VI. 18), he claims that the Cyclopes were Sicily's original inhabitants. In fact, the earliest human habitation of the island seems to have commenced around 10,000 B.C. Cave carvings in Addaura, near present-day Palermo, date from about 8,000 B.C. ("Best").

As an island, Sicily could well have promoted dwarfism; the same is true for other islands on which the bones of the elephants have been found. These include Mediterranean ones such as Crete, Cyprus, Malta, Sardinia, and Delos, and the Channel Islands, off of southern California. During the Pleistocene, while the seas were low, the animals probably wandered out to these areas, which were not islands at the time, but connected to the mainland. However, when the Ice Age ended and the polar caps began melting, the oceans rose, stranding

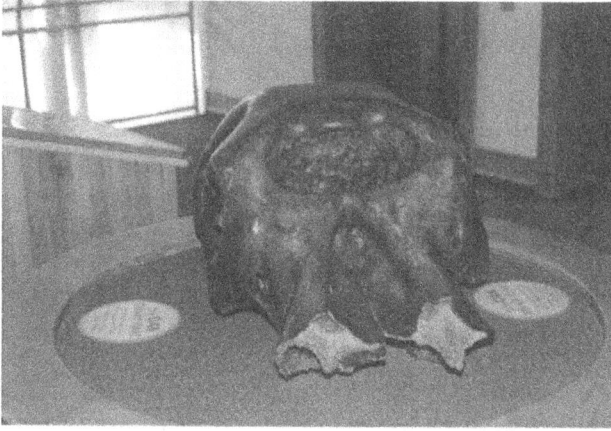

Figure 1.6 Mastodon skull, with the large trunk cavity in front. (The actual eye-sockets are on the sides of the skull.) Photo by Crazycomputers, 2010. Wikimedia Commons.

certain populations of elephants, along with other mammals, and eventually retarding the growth of their descendants.

Another piece of supporting evidence for Abel's supposition is that the term "Cyclopes" means "round eyes" or "circle eyes"; the cavity in the faces of the dwarf elephants is truly circular, as opposed to mammoths and mastodons, who have elliptically shaped openings (Figure 1.6). Then again, dwarf elephants were just six feet tall at the shoulder, while the other species were considerably larger, about double this size, and thus, perhaps, more likely to arouse tales of colossal figures. Yet although the mastodon and mammoth eye-sockets are more oval-shaped than circular, the mastodon teeth, as noted, seem to imply carnivory and lend their skulls an appearance that could suggest a malevolent, humanoid grin. In any event, no single species is required to explain the origin of the Cyclopes, as there are plenty of elephantine remains of all sorts deposited throughout the Mediterranean and Aegean. And of course bone discoveries from different species could have been combined to arrive at a "composite" monster. Once more, however, to risk overemphasis of a key point, not one type is required; imagination alone would suffice.

Nevertheless, the geomythical questions are fascinating to contemplate even if they cannot be answered definitively. And we do have some plausible cases from antiquity in which the skeleton of a large animal, probably a rhino or mammoth, was misidentified as an outsized man. For instance, in *The Aeneid,* Book II, Virgil describes the sack of Troy, when the Greeks finally penetrate the city by hiding in the Trojan Horse, then emerging at night to carry out a thrilling sneak attack. During the melee, the Trojan king Priam is brutally stabbed to death at Zeus's altar by Pyrrhus, one of the invading Greeks. After recounting the event, Virgil provides Priam with a curious epitaph: "On the distant shore/The vast trunk [of the slain king] *headless* lies without a name" (ll. 728–29; my emphasis). The description is peculiar since although the scene of the king's slaying is graphically detailed, there is no mention of him being decapitated, only stabbed. Moreover, Priam clearly dies *within* the walls of Troy, which is later burned to the ground. Hence, the notion of Priam's headless corpse somehow surviving to the time when Virgil was writing, hundreds of years later, and lying outside the city walls on the beach, seems odd.

One geomythical possibility is that the headless trunk described here is not Priam's. Instead, it could be the bones of a large mammal, which died at the water's edge, ages prior to the Trojan War, and was later exposed during a storm and misclassified as a gigantic human (Burbery, "Geomythology"). Mayor offers an example of a similarly creative mistake regarding the Greek warrior Ajax, who towered over his fellow soldiers: "According to Homeric myth, Ajax's grave was on the headland of Rhoeteum, where the Greek ships had landed to attack Troy" ("First" 115). She goes on to speculate that "[b]ones big enough to be worthy of the mighty Ajax would most likely belong to a Miocene mastodon or rhino," and notes that Troy's crumbling coastline regularly exposes such remains. In addition, she cites Philostratus's record of Ajax's corpse, set forth in his book *On Heroes,* where the body is said to have measured a staggering fifteen feet in length. Again, the size here suggests something animalian, not human. Other discoveries in antiquity include the supposed remnants of Hector, Orestes, Achilles, and Antaeus (Mayor, "First" 113 269). All were reputed to be large, even colossal in stature; all invite geomythical analysis.[2]

Volcanic Geomyths

After Odysseus and his men escape the Cyclops's cave, they rush to their ship and quickly put out from shore. However, because he is still furious at Polyphemus for slaughtering his men, Odysseus taunts him from the boat. Hence, the mariners do not depart unscathed: the outraged giant, though blind, hurls boulders in their direction with sickening accuracy, nearly capsizing the boat. And when Odysseus reveals his true name, the ogre invokes a curse on him that is fulfilled by Polyphemus's father, Poseidon, who delays Odysseus's homecoming by ten years.

This element of the Cyclops narrative provides a useful segue into volcanic geomyths. These may have been influenced by some of the planet's major eruptions, including Thera, cited earlier; Ilopango (El Salvador), in or around 535 A.D.; an unidentified volcano near the tropics, around 539 A.D.; Tambora (Indonesia), in 1815; and Mt. Etna's ongoing eruptions in eastern Sicily. These blasts are among the most cataclysmic natural events of all time, and it is not surprising to see that they have been linked with events ranging from global cooling and the creation of literary and artistic masterpieces to more far-fetched ones such as the defeat of Napoleon at Waterloo, and even the birth of human consciousness.[3]

Returning to Odysseus's flight from Polyphemus, there is a group of rocks known as the Cyclopean Isles, located just off Sicily's east coast, which are alleged to be the boulders hurled at the trickster by the enraged giant. Given that they protrude dramatically from the water, they might indeed look as if they came from elsewhere. Hence, this aspect of the Cyclopean narrative may constitute a geomythical explanation for their seemingly alien presence. Yet, according to Dorothy Vitaliano, they are, in fact, leftovers of "small plugs of basaltic rock" that were eroded by the waves, though still exposed enough to draw attention to themselves (139). She cites the Cyclops's action as an example of an etiological geomyth, an after-the-fact "tall tale" with no actual eyewitnesses. Yet she also allows for the possibility of a euhemeristic account of the narrative; that is, the story could have been inspired by the "volcanic bombs and blocks of all dimensions" that are seemingly "thrown" from Etna during its eruptions (140).

As noted in the introduction, the Titanomachy was almost certainly inspired by the eruption of Thera (Figure 1.7). Like Mott Greene, Vitaliano also sees a link here; however, she focuses less on the blast itself and more on one of its effects, that is, a possible tsunami. Hence, she invokes not the Titanomachy (Zeus v. the Titans) but the war succeeding it, that is, the Gigantomachy (The Olympians v. the Giants), which results in the "dragonscapes" identified by Daniel Ogden, discussed earlier. To set up her account, Vitaliano cites a passage from Hesiod's *Theogony* that describes this duel: "And the heat from [Zeus and Typhon] gripped the purple sea, the heat of thunder and lightning and of fire from such a monster, the heat of fiery storm-winds and flaming thunderbolt. And the whole earth and

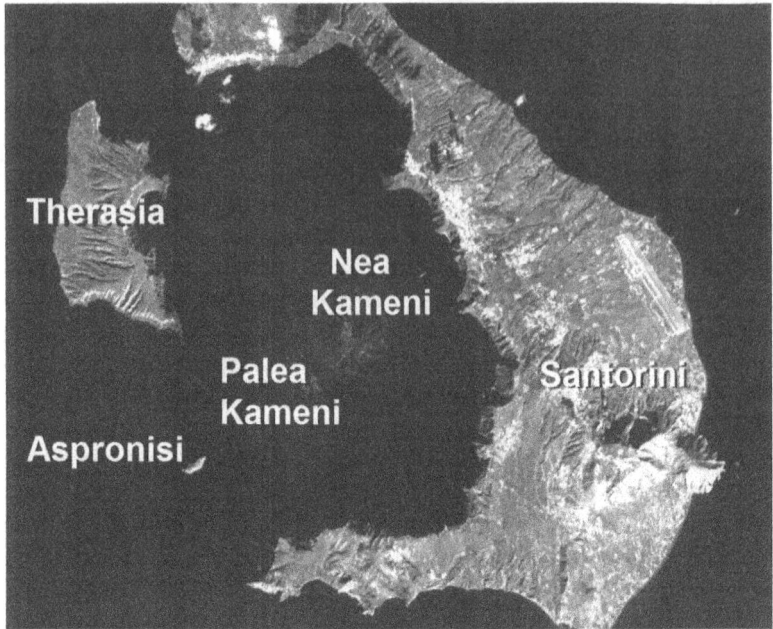

Figure 1.7 Satellite image of the Santorini Islands archipelago, 2000. Thera is
    the large eastern island on the right. EOS Photo/NASA. Wikimedia
    Images.

firmament and sea boiled. And long waves spreading out in circles
went seething over the headlands, and unquenchable earthquakes
broke out" (250).

    The reference to "long waves," she argues, may be a link with Thera.
Vitaliano admits that "[t]sunamis are *not* normally associated with
eruptions, usually only with submarine eruptions and with very few of
those, at that" (250; my emphasis). Yet she declares that "the one
eruption of antiquity which may have generated a large tsunami, if the
collapse of the caldera was sudden, is precisely the Bronze Age eruption of [Thera]!" (250). And in fact, since Vitaliano wrote these words
in 1973, research on volcanic tsunamis has grown (Hunter).

    Vitaliano, in addition, touches on another potential Theran fable,
that of Jason and the Argonauts. In it, Jason, king of Iolcos, leads his
crew (which includes Hercules) to win the Golden Fleece from
Chrysomallos, a ram with wings and a golden coat. They sail to
Colchis (situated today on the eastern shore of the Black Sea), where

the ram is kept, and succeed with the help of Medea, daughter to the king of Colchis. She is also the niece of the sorceress Circe and is thus able to lull to sleep, with narcotics, the dragon that guards the Fleece. Once they obtain the treasure, the crew leaves, and Medea, having fallen in love with Jason, accompanies them.

On their way home, they encounter many adventures, including one with Talos, a bronze automaton who guards Europa, mother of Minos. She has been confined to Crete by Zeus, who has tasked Talos with circling the island three times a day to ward off would-be invaders. While Talos initially refuses to let the *Argo* land, Medea eventually gains Talos's trust by promising him immortality. He relents, and they come ashore, whereupon she pulls a nail out of Talos's foot. This action causes his lifeblood, called ichor, to run out. Shortly thereafter, he dies. Following this episode, the Argonauts set sail once more and are soon plunged into "black chaos coming down from the sky, or some other darkness rising from the inmost recesses of the earth" (qtd. in Vitaliano 249) and become completely disoriented. In desperation, they pray to Apollo, who eventually guides them to the island of Anafi, one of the Greeks isles. Interestingly, Anafi is situated just 20 kilometers east of Santorini.

Vitaliano proposes that the account of the Anafi landing might be based on the actual voyage of "some Greek ship, venturing close to [Thera] during a lull in the eruption ... Such a ship might land on Anafi just by luck after losing its bearings; having survived ... the crew would provide a detail to be worked into the story of Jason and the Argonauts by later story tellers" (249). Geoscientists K.J. Evans and Floyd McCoy complicate the picture somewhat, however, in a remarkable 2020 paper. They cite evidence that Thera's main explosion was preceded by smaller tremors, which would have alerted residents of nearby settlements, including those living on Akrotiri, a small village on the southern end of the island. As a result, these Therans would have had time to escape and row away from the blast, a conjecture supported by the fact that no human remains have been discovered under the thick layer of tephra, that is, the debris ejected by an eruption.

On the other hand, Evans and McCoy also note that "there is insufficient evidence of major influxes [at this time] of new people with Theran crafts at archaeological sites in the Aegean" (2). Moreover, the blast produced extremely hot water-flows known as "pyroclastic density currents"; such currents "can traverse the sea surface for long distances" (7). Evans and McCoy thus reach a grisly conclusion: would-be escapees were "incinerated at sea" (7). Hence, it is possible that passing boats like the *Argo* also would have been destroyed, as Anafi is within the range of the pyroclastic current flow. Nevertheless, if the Argonauts somehow did manage to survive while most neighboring boats did not, the trauma of the ordeal certainly could have inspired a memorable tale.

Thera and the Biblical Plagues

In addition to accounting for mythical narratives, the Thera eruption has been adduced to explain the biblical plagues in Exodus. Angelos Galanopoulous was the first to propose the connection in a 1964 article. Vitaliano added further evidence in her 1973 book, pointing out that the prevailing winds blow southeast, allowing the possibility that thick tephra from the blast drifted 500 or so miles to Egypt, thereby creating intense darkness: the ninth plague. Such blackness, notably, is recorded not only in the book of Exodus but also in Egyptian sources.

Other researchers, however, contend that the timing does not fit. De Boer and Sanders's assessment, published in 2002, exemplifies a common scholarly view: "Biblical scholars ... generally place the Exodus in the fifteenth century B.C.E., whereas the eruption ... most likely occurred much *earlier*, in the seventeenth century" ("Volcanoes" 69; my emphasis). In this scenario, the proposed date for the Exodus would occur almost exactly two centuries after the Minoan event. And while volcanic debris from large volcanoes can remain in the atmosphere for years, it seldom lasts a century, let alone two.

However, more recent findings suggest the events were much closer, chronologically. The older view relies heavily on a bible passage, 1 Kings 6:1, which in the King James Version reads as follows: "And it came to pass in the four hundred and eightieth year after the children of Israel were come out of the land of Egypt, in the fourth year of Solomon's reign over Israel ... that he began to build the house of the LORD." Assuming that the fourth year of Solomon's time on the throne would have been in about 960 B.C., working backward has led scholars to place the Exodus at around 1440 B.C., since 960 + 480 = 1440.

Even so, in her 2009 study of the geological background of the Exodus, Barbara Sivertsen, long-time editor of the *Journal of Geology*, argues that the two dates—the eruption and Exodus—were essentially simultaneous and happened earlier in 1628 B.C. She arrives at the date of the Exodus by taking the ancient Jewish historian Josephus's work *Antiquities of the Jews* as a mostly reliable text (Sivertsen does flag a counting error committed by him). Her discussion resists easy summary, but several figures stand out. The date of the (first) Jewish temple's destruction is generally accepted to be about 586 B.C. In addition, according to Josephus—and *contrary* to 1 Kings—572 years passed between the Exodus and the beginning of the temple's construction, and it was destroyed 470 years later. Proceeding in reverse chronological order, Sivertsen starts with the 586 B.C. figure, then moves back 470 years (the beginning of its building), which takes her to 1056 B.C. (586 + 470). She then goes back 572 *more* years, which, again, is the number of years alleged by Josephus to have passed between the Exodus and the temple building. That is 1056 + 572. The figure that she arrives at, using Josephus, is 1628 B.C. (586 + 470 + 572) (4–5).

As for scientific attempts to date the explosion, in 2013, Panagiotakopulu et al. made a compelling case for a period between 1744–1538 B.C., using an innovative method: they examined the charred remains of bean weevils, a pest common in the Bronze Age settlement of Akrotiri, which is situated, as mentioned earlier, on Thera's southern tip. In fact, Akrotiri is sometimes called "the Aegean Pompeii" since, at the time of their respective eruptions, both settlements were rapidly engulfed by falling ash and debris, yet paradoxically preserved thereby. Both have yielded many remarkable artifacts underneath the tephra, including, in Akrotiri's case, jars of wheat with the burned insects in them.

Regarding Sivertsen's use of the scientific data, she notes that "for most of the twentieth century, archaeologists placed [the event] at about 1500 B.C.," but adds that more recent carbon dating techniques have pushed the date earlier (23). Since then, some of the most compelling evidence yet adduced has come from Thera itself. In addition to the scorched weevils, there were also seeds buried in sealed jars, which were recovered from the eruption; they have been dated at 1660–13 B.C., with a subrange of 1639–16 (24). Also discovered in the tephra was an olive branch; it was almost certainly alive at the time of the event and produced a dating range of 1627–1600 (23). Furthermore, those dates can be narrowed by evidence from several Greenlandic ice cores and by the fact that tree-rings in European and North American sites "record a growth anomaly thought to be the product of a volcanic eruption—1628 B.C.E." (24).

Sivertsen then builds on this evidence to link the Thera blast to the Egyptian plagues. The turning of the Nile to blood, for instance, could have been caused by a "red algal 'bloom'" (39) brought ashore by the tsunami waves from the eruption. (This phenomenon is known as a "volcanic tsunami," cited earlier, and may account for a full quarter of all tsunami deaths [Hunter par. 14]). The plagues would have proceeded in a cascading manner, with the next one (frog swarms) occurring when the frogs' freshwater habitats would have been contaminated. The gnat infestation, she believes, could be a primitive attempt to explain what she calls "biting dust": "Dust usually comes from the ground, and so it does in this present version of the story when, becoming transformed into gnats, it was the only way to make sense of biting dust." This dust, in fact, "came from the air in the first winds that carried fine ash from the initial stages of the Plinian eruption cloud to the [Nile] Delta" (39). And so on.

While Sivertsen's claims are intriguing, they should be treated with caution. For one thing, it can be risky to read the biblical accounts at face value without full attention to their metaphorical, literary elements. To her credit, she recognizes the oral roots of the biblical texts and the ways the orality could have shaped and even altered the narrative. For instance, her concluding chapter, "The Formation of the Exodus Tradition," identifies certain inconsistencies in the narrative and proposes a two-part Exodus, as well as, interestingly, the existence of two Moses figures (148–51). Other sections in her book, however, treat the texts as relatively straightforward history. This attitude is, as we saw, evident in the discussion of the plagues. Matt Kaplan accepts the possible link with the eruption yet takes Sivertsen to task for failing to grasp the metaphorical facets of the episodes:

> The plagues are the quintessential narrative fragment. With a sequence running from one to ten and set progression of horrible events, they were the perfect sort of thing for an oral teller of tales to have learned after a real catastrophe, like the Thera eruption, and then dropped into oral stories in the centuries that followed. (93)

In addition, Sivertsen's specification of one particular year (1628 B.C.)—in fact, the exact *month* (February)—for an event that occurred millennia ago demands a high standard of proof, of course. In fairness to her, other researchers have also tried to nail down a precise date, since, as Pearson et al. remark, in a study that came out the same year (2009) as Sivertsen's book, "it is the exact date of the eruption which continues to raise major controversy" (1206). They used dendrochemical analysis, which is the study of what tree rings reveal about air pollution in that tree's environment. They also employed microscopy and spectroscopy, motivated by the fact that "if ... a connection [between tree-ring anomalies and the Thera eruption] could be proved it would be of major interdisciplinary significance," and would "open up the possibility of a precise date for a key archaeological, geological and environmental marker horizon" (1206). While the results were not conclusive, they may have paved the way for future research.

Non-western Volcanic Tales

Probably the most well-known non-Theran volcanic myths are the Hawaiian legends of Pele, goddess of fire and volcanoes, and her feuds with her sisters. One version involves an ongoing conflict between Pele and Namakaokahai, goddess of the sea. According to this tale, Pele first came to the islands to escape her sister, starting at the top of the archipelago, in what is now Kauai, and working her way down, in a southeastern direction. She needed to keep moving since, at each island, she would dig a fire pit, only to have it fill up with ocean water. When Pele came to Maui, she thought she had found a home, at last, having succeeded in creating the volcano Haleakala. However, its smoke alerted Namakaokahai to Pele's presence, and another fight ensued. This time, Pele was destroyed, with "her bones [being] scattered along the coast" (Vitaliano 107), yet her unvanquished spirit hovered for a time in clouds of smoke over Mauna Loa. When it became clear that her sister was no longer able to harass her, Pele returned to earth, dug her final fire pit in the Kilauea caldera (108), and resides there to this day.

Regarding the Pele narratives, geoscientists Jelle Zeilinga de Boer and Donald T. Sanders declare that "there are remarkable similarities between the origin of the Hawaiian Islands as explained by plate tectonics and the mythological explanations of how the fire goddess Pele came to live in Hawaii" (32). These include the fact that the islands' development parallels the goddess's route. That is, proceeding in a northwest to southeast direction, each island is younger than the previous one (Vitaliano 109). Another geological feature is evident in the episode in which Pele allegedly dug a pit at the site known today as Diamond Head (Figure 1.8). "That spot," note de Boer and Sanders, is a "landmark ... now understood to be the eroded remains of an ancient, extinct volcano comprising many layers of compacted volcanic ash and fragments of a limestone reef that was penetrated by the volcano's upwelling magma" (33). And when Pele strikes water during one of her digs, they note that probably "what happened in fact is that groundwater or perhaps seawater penetrated into the magma chamber, flashed to steam, and created an explosive eruption" (33).

Another rich group of volcanic myths comes from Java, an island that is part of Indonesia. Formed almost completely from volcanic

Figure 1.8 Diamond Head, Hawaii. Photo by Eric Tessmer, 2019. Wikimedia Commons.

processes, Java possesses nearly 50 active volcanoes—including the notorious Krakatau—and its fables contrast markedly with the Pele narratives. The latter, as noted, record the ongoing feud between Pele and her sisters and were almost certainly inspired by lava flows, earthquakes, and tsunamis. By contrast, the Javanese stories are often gentler, and at times, wonderfully quirky. Boer's discussion of them is doubly valuable: not only is he a geologist, he was raised in one of the country's (inactive) volcanoes, according to the dust jacket of his 2004 book, *Volcanoes in Human History*. One highlight of his volcano survey is Mt. Merapi, located in central Java. It allegedly supports a ghost kingdom, complete with "palace, rulers, soldiers, servants, and farmers" (184). And in what might be called a proto-post-colonial element, while most of the spirits on Merapi are Javanese, one version depicts a European (Baron Kasender) serving as the kingdom's "gardener spirit" (184).

In addition, de Boer points outs that "the Javanese recognize the beneficial aspects of volcanism." For instance, Merapi's ghost monarch frequently makes love with the ocean queen, and the volcano's eruptions are seen as "spectral ejaculations" which "flow downstream to fertilize [her]" (184). He then translates this fable geologically: mud and ash from the volcano "fertilize coastal waters and increase the yield of fish and other seafood" (184). A 2007 study published in *Geophysical Research Letters* could support this alleged link. It points out that volcanic ash in Costa Rica, Japan, and Alaska—like Java, all located on the Pacific Ring of Fire—has been found to enhance phytoplankton activity, a result that could potentially multiply the fish harvest. Moreover, they comment on the divergent tones of the Pele and Java myths in terms of lava flow. In Hawaii, it is rare for flowing lava not to reach the sea, and when it does so, "the molten rock reacts explosively with seawater," thereby inspiring tales of violent discord. In Java, however, since many volcanoes are far inland, their lava seldom make it to the ocean (185).

Secondary Effects of Volcanic Myths

As we touched on briefly above, in Norse myth, there is an episode known as Fimbulvetr (Old Norse for "Terrible Winter"). It marks the beginning of the end for Thor, Odin, Loki, and the other gods. Fimbulvetr is a period of three years, in which it is continuously winter, with none of the other three seasons taking place. Snow falls from every direction during this time, and many living things perish. Fimbulvetr inaugurates Ragnarök, traditionally translated as "Twilight of the Gods," during which time anarchy breaks out on earth, with brother fighting brother, sister attacking sister, and sexual license running rampant. Ragnarök culminates in a worldwide, Armageddon-style battle, in which the gods are slain: for instance, Odin is devoured by Fenrir, the colossal wolf, and Thor collapses while clashing with the great serpent, Jörmungandr. The sun is shrouded in darkness, and the earth plunges into the sea.

    These stories may have come about in response to what might be called the second-hand effects of volcanic activity. As opposed to myths that are directly indebted to immediate effects like lava flows, these and other narratives appear to be based on post-eruption events such as volcanic winter, in which vast amounts of ash and debris, ejected into the stratosphere, block the sun. Researchers have sought a weather event that could have influenced their composition. Geologist W.H. Berger, for instance, approvingly cites H.H. Lamb's proposal that ties the Norse fables to the Thera volcanic eruption. As Berger notes, the proposal "gets us back 3500 years [that is, to about 1500 B.C.] for this important element in Norse myth" (127). Berger also claims that stories about a key Norse god, Thor, are "ancient," and could have originated "well before the time of [the historian] Tacitus" (56 A.D. - 120 A.D.) (127). However, one considerable problem with these proposed dates is that Norse myth was not written down until the mythographer Snorri Sturluson did so in the 13th century A.D., in the *Prose Edda*, the mother lode of Norse tales. Snorri quotes a number of Norse poets in the *Edda*, and they worked in the relatively recent past; Eyvind Skaldaspillir, for instance, wrote in the 10th century A.D., as did Thjodolf of Hvin (Byock 135, 136). Of course, oral tradition could have been operative for many centuries prior to Snorri's compilation, yet it seems more likely that a date closer to the 13th century is called for. By failing to consider a more recent origin, Berger and Lamb overlook more recent catastrophes that would have been sufficiently traumatic to provoke mythmaking.

Two plausible candidates are the extreme weather events of A.D. 535–36 and A.D. 539-40. Both resulted in widespread crop failure, prolonged dimming of the sun, global cooling, and the Plague of Justinian, a pandemic that claimed 25–50 million lives. These and other such catastrophes are well attested in writers such as Procopius (A.D. 500–65), in tree-rings, and in ice cores. The 535–36 catastrophe may have been triggered by a volcanic eruption, possibly Mt. Ilopango, in modern day El Salvador. The 539-40 cataclysm possibly resulted from another eruption, this one in the tropics. In their 2015 *Nature* paper, Sigl et al. present their findings on ice core chronology to support their thesis that the 6th century global crisis may have come about because of this one-two punch, that is, one eruption followed by another shortly thereafter (5). These explosions appear to have injected so much debris into the atmosphere that people-groups around the world were affected.

If we accept this theory, it could also provide insight into Norse narratives such as the death of Balder. The son of Odin, Balder was extraordinarily handsome and fair-haired, in keeping with his status as the god of light and joy. Yet one night, he began having nightmares about some impending misfortune that would soon befall him. When Odin went to the underworld to inquire about his son's future, he learned to his sorrow that Balder would be arriving there shortly. On his return, Odin broke the terrible news to Balder's mother. Once she absorbed the shock, she became determined to defy the prophecy and protect her son at all costs. She visited every living thing in the world and obtained a promise from each one not to harm Balder. All except one, that is; she did not get the mistletoe to comply. (This oversight is sometimes explained by the fact that mistletoe seems innocuous since it grows high in trees and consists of small, soft leaves.) (Figure 1.9)

Meanwhile, Balder lived as normally as he could, and one day he and his brothers were roughhousing. The brothers hurled rocks and sticks at Balder, who was delighted—unlike the nursery rhyme, sticks and stones could *not* break his bones. However, when Loki saw what was happening, he tricked Balder's blind brother Höd into throwing a stick at Balder as well, with this fatal difference: Loki provided Höd with a dart made of a sharpened mistletoe branch. It hit the mark, killing Balder, and he went down into the underworld.

Figure 1.9 Mistletoe plant in white poplar. Photo by Andrew Dunn, 2004. Wikimedia Commons.

Even though the Vikings had a sun-goddess (Sól), the death of Balder, the light god, may reflect an eclipsing or shrouding of the sun. On a related note, there is intriguing archaeological evidence that the Vikings' sun worship ceased permanently around A.D. 535–36—the time of the first eruption of Ilopango. Researchers have discovered a spike in ritual depositions of gold at this time throughout Europe. These were deposits that seem to have been intended not as attempts to hide the treasure till it could be recovered later, but rather, as valuables to be placed ritually and permanently in the ground. Commenting on these finds, archaeologist Morton Axboe remarks,

a significant number of Migration-period [5th-century A.D. onwards] gold hoards seem to be … 'official' offerings made by the [Viking] elite on behalf of the community. These finds include gold bracteates [medals or medallions], massive arm- and neck-rings, scabbard mounts and silver-gilt square-headed brooches; in other words, heavily status-bearing objects, some of which also can be assumed to have had amuletic functions. It must have been a very serious matter to sacrifice such things; they were not only valuables but also expressions of one's social role and status, as well as powerful protective amulets. (187)

During the same period, there appears to be a corresponding decrease in the use of sun emblems—including the sun-wheel, *sólarhvél*, which is closely related to the swastika—in Viking culture (Gräslund & Price 439). One possible explanation is that the Norsemen grew worried at the sun's darkening and tried to appease the deity by placing the sun-based metal, gold, into the sacred sites. Eventually, however, as the darkness wore on and months turned into years, they finally abandoned sun-worship. And they may have invented the story of Ragnarök to explain the demise of the sun deity as well as the others. Indeed, Gräslund speculates that the very term Ragnarök ("Twilight of the Gods") might be based on the sun's veiling.

We can also venture some guesses as to how another massive eruption might have affected writers and poets in more recent times, even those who lived far from the blast site, by studying the aftermath of the explosion of Tambora in April 1815, the strongest recorded eruption in recorded history. Its VEI measured 7. For comparison, Krakatau's blast registered 6 on the VEI, while Mt. St. Helens's was rated at 5.

Possibly the most famous alleged effect of Tambora from a literary perspective is the novel *Frankenstein*. The work was conceived when the poet Lord Byron proposed a ghost-story contest to a small group of intimates in Geneva, Switzerland. The group included Mary Shelley, author of *Frankenstein*, and poet Percy Shelley, Mary's husband, as well as the physician John Polidori. Due to inclement weather, they had gone indoors during what would normally be the warmest time of the year, in 1816, the so-called "year without a summer." As with the Ilopango and Thera eruptions, ash deposition was widespread and served to lower temperatures around the globe, though in the case of Tambora, perhaps less so than has been thought. The novel's murky, gothic setting could be indebted to the unseasonably cold, wet conditions Mary Shelley was experiencing with her friends during its composition.

Moreover, the novel is structured around a frame narrative, based on a series of letters from one character (John Walton) to his sister, and he is writing to her from the Arctic regions. Walton has traveled north to make a name for himself, either by discovering the fabled Northwest Passage or the North Pole. The Passage was a trading route from Europe to Asia by way of the Arctic Ocean, and the search for it took on a new urgency during this period. Such a quest might initially seem counter-intuitive since Tambora caused global *cooling* throughout much of the world, as the sulfur dioxide it ejected into the atmosphere led to glaciation. Hence, the ice in these regions would, presumably, grow even thicker and thus block access.

However, in keeping with an Earth System approach, it is worth recalling what NASA climate scientist Alan Buis points out, that "global surface temperatures are a 'noisy' signal," by which he means that they are "always varying to some degree due to constant interactions between the various components of our complex Earth system (e.g., land, ocean, air, ice)" ("Nope"). In the case of Tambora, it chilled much of the planet but, surprisingly, warmed up the Arctic regions due to "wind circulation and North Atlantic currents" (Wood par. 12). Moreover, in 1817, news began to reach England of "a remarkable loss of sea ice around Greenland"; at the same time, enormous icebergs appeared as far south as New York Harbor (Wood par. 13). Such events stimulated both fictional and real-life exploration of the Arctic region. Today, as the Arctic warms, the Passage is, in theory, open. However, Katie Peek notes that "in practice, lingering ice is so unpredictable that a crossing remains risky and expensive" (80). Today, the Northwest Passage effectively exists simply because most of the ice in this region has melted.

Other writers who reacted artistically to the cataclysm include Lord Byron, whose contributions included "A Fragment," which later became the basis for Polidori's *The Vampyre*, the precursor to *Dracula*. Byron also composed a poem, "Darkness," which evokes the surreal weather powerfully: "I had a dream, which was not all a dream./The bright sun was extinguish'd, and the stars / Did wander darkling in the eternal space ..." (1–3). Perhaps most striking was the way the volcano helped to inspire what many literary scholars regard as the "most perfect poem in English" (Birkerts 175), that is, John Keats's "To Autumn." Its elegance is evident in the opening lines, where the speaker personifies autumn: "Season of mists and mellow fruitfulness, / Close bosom-friend of the maturing sun; / Conspiring with him how to load and bless / With fruit the vines that round the thatch-eves run ..." (1–4). The fact that the volcano helped to bring about such a masterfully constructed work is ironic, given that Tambora claimed about 100,000 human lives, making it the most destructive eruption in history.

Here is the poem's probable genesis: in 1819, Keats strolled along the River Itchen, located in southeastern England, then later described the scene to his friend John Reynolds, as well as the vista's influence on the poem's composition: "How beautiful the season is now – How fine the air. A temperate sharpness about it [...] I never lik'd stubble fields so much as now [...] Somehow a stubble plain looks warm – in the same way that some pictures look warm – this struck me so much in my Sunday's walk that I composed upon it." Scholars have speculated that Keats, along with many in the post-Tambora world, was especially appreciative of the lovely, clear weather that returned in 1819 after several years of climatic instability brought on by the eruption (Bate 439–40).

Even so, while these potential links are fascinating to contemplate, as so often with geomythology, we must take them with a grain of salt. In their 2016 study, Brönnimann and Krämer suggest that other factors besides Tambora played a larger part in the cooling in and around Geneva. This study notes that "temperatures in Geneva and surrounding areas were ca. 2.5–3° (Celsius) lower in the summer of 1816 during the period 1799–1821 (21)." However, they also assert that "[i]n all, [only] around 0.7–1° Celsius of the temperature decrease can be attributed directly or indirectly to the Tambora eruption" (21). Thus, it would appear that further research is needed to test the alleged connections between the volcanic event and these outcomes. Otherwise, the "Tambora effect," viewed uncritically, could run the risk of becoming a new geomyth of the etiological variety.

Notes

1 According to Nelson, an understanding of the "development of the embryological development of the vertebrate face [suggests that] the fronto-nasal process … pushes forward and downward to produce the nose and the middle portion of the upper jaw, including the philtrum. The paired maxillary … and mandibular … processes grow forward from the sides of the head and join in the midline to produce the remainder of the upper jaw and the lower jaw respectively. The eyes are thereby enclosed on either side of the head between the frontal nasal and maxillary processes during the development. When … but a single eye is formed during very early development, this single eye occupies the space in the midline in front. As such, this single eye then prevents the frontal-nasal process from growing according to its normal pattern and the nose resulting from it thereupon remains *above* the single eye." Hence, had the mythmakers based the ogre's appearance on actual cases, the nose would have been over the eye (160–61; my emphasis).

2 Regarding fossil giants in ancient Jewish history, see Fine and Fine, "Rabbinic Paleontology: Jewish Encounters with Fossil Giants in Roman Antiquity."

3 For a discussion of Tambora's impact on Napoleon, see Starr. Regarding the claim that the Santorini eruption led to the birth of human consciousness, see Jaynes.

2 Universal Geomyths (Part II)

Flood Fables

In or around A.D. 767, Guru Rinpoche, the "Precious Master," brought Buddhism to Tibet. The story of how he did so is captured in a memorable folk tale. There was a lake, high up in the mountains of northwest Tibet, and held captive by a formidable lake-demon (Montgomery 5). When the Master arrived, he took on the demon, and a tremendous struggle ensued. Eventually, the Guru prevailed, the water was released, and the lake was drained; at the same time, the villagers in the area were given access to rich farmland. And many, impressed by Rinpoche's feat, converted to Buddhism.

Readers today may smile at the story, but once again, geomythology hints at a real natural event behind it. American geomorphologist David Montgomery argues that the fable anticipated his official discovery of an ancient, natural dam in the Brahmaputra River (in northwest Tibet), made of dirt and ice, which descended from an elevation of about 25,000 feet, to block the headwaters of the river and create a massive lake. It later broke, sending, in Montgomery's words, "a wall of water down the deepest gorge on earth" ("A geologist's"). Such a dramatic event could easily have inspired the victory of one spiritual being over another. Indeed, Montgomery subsequently learned that the local villagers already knew about the flood even before he broached the subject as it was enshrined in the legend about Guru Rinpoche. One farmer's wife, in fact, pointed out an area high up on the mountain wall, marking a spot where, supposedly, three boats were once stranded ("A geologist's").

Flood tales like this are among the oldest stories on earth and the most prevalent. They can be found on nearly all continents, with the partial exception of Africa, yet the dearth of flood narratives there is not difficult to explain: for example, up until 1960, when the Aswan

Dam was built, Egypt had an annual, predictable flood event when the Nile crested. It did so, not disastrously, but "gently and predictably," as Vitaliano notes, as do other main rivers on the continent (164). Hence, such flooding tended to lack the kind of trauma that seems to have inspired most geomyths.

In western culture, the most famous inundation tales are Noah's flood, of course, and the one depicted in the ancient Mesopotamian poem, *The Epic of Gilgamesh*. Whether these narratives contain any truth is a question that has inspired considerable debate. In his research papers, 2012 book *The Rocks Don't Lie: A Geologist Investigates Noah's Flood*, and TED talk, Montgomery once again argues for the essential trustworthiness of these myths. Like many scientists, he notes that he initially regarded the legends as "fairy tales, rooted in superstition," before coming to believe that "flood stories from around the world are grounded in reality" (176).

Regarding the biblical inundation, Montgomery favorably cites the controversial Black Sea Deluge Hypothesis, which we will discuss shortly. Montgomery also contends that the Noah narrative in Genesis inspired early scientists like Nicholas Steno (1638–86), the grandfather of geology (and later Roman Catholic bishop), who turned to the story to complement his field findings. In fact, Montgomery argues that "you might even say that Noah's flood served as the first geological theory." In a similar fashion, William Buckland (1784–1856), inaugural Professor of Geology at Oxford, initially saw full congruence between geology and the notion of a worldwide flood, though he later changed his views as he studied the earth. And as Montgomery shows, "by the end of the 19th century, scientists had laid to rest the notion of a universal flood."

In *The Rocks Don't Lie*, Montgomery helps readers grasp why ancient peoples tended to believe in global floods, given the scale of the bodies of water they knew. Lake Agassiz, for instance, which was formed when the North American ice sheet melted, was once the largest lake in the world, area-wise. It was about the size Hudson Bay is today and would have dwarfed the entire Great Lakes region (214) (Figure 2.1). As Montgomery points out, "[i]t's nearly impossible today to understand how gargantuan ancient floods were, because so many of the world's rivers have been engineered to reduce [them]" (153).

Given the sheer number of flood tales, we will briefly consider just the Noah deluge and *Gilgamesh* and briefly touch on *The Atra-Hasis Epic* as well. The latter is named for its hero (his name means exceedingly wise), and tells the story of a figure who builds a boat to escape a flood. He puts his family and his animals inside of it. *Atra-Hasis* probably gave

50   *Universal Geomyths (Part II)*

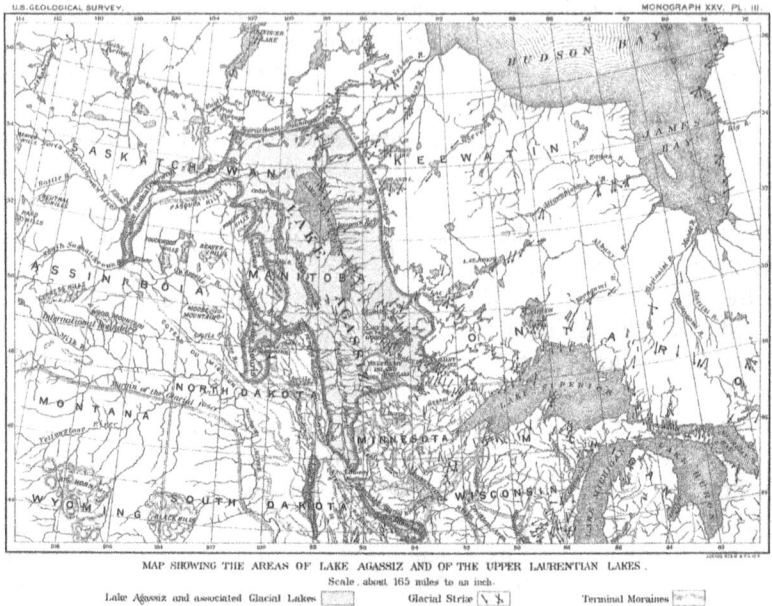

MAP SHOWING THE AREAS OF LAKE AGASSIZ AND OF THE UPPER LAURENTIAN LAKES.
Scale, about 165 miles to an inch.
Lake Agassiz and associated Glacial Lakes ▯   Glacial Striæ ▯   Terminal Moraines ▯

Figure 2.1 Lake Agassiz (left center) in relation to Hudson Bay and the Great
Lakes. U.S. Geological Survey map, 1985. Wikimedia Commons.

Gilgamesh its flood story, recounted in Book XI of *Gilgamesh* (Tigay 25).
Genesis may have, in turn, been affected by *Gilgamesh*, which is based on
a real ruler, Gilgamesh, who was on the Sumerian throne of the city of
Uruk between 2800 and 2500 B.C. As for dating these works, scholars
continue to contest the details, but the rough contours are these: *Atra-
Hasis* was set down in writing during the reign of Ammi-Saduqa
(grandson of Hammurabi, reputed creator of the Code of Hammurabi),
that is, from 1646–26 B.C., though its oral roots are much earlier.
Gilgamesh itself may have been composed around 2000 B.C., while the
earliest that Genesis could have been either composed or compiled is
around 1400 B.C.

It is possible that the Genesis author/editor decided to borrow certain
elements from the Sumerian text, perhaps in recognition of its antiquity
and cultural authority. The Sumerians lived in Mesopotamia, south of
modern-day Baghdad (Iraq), beginning in the fourth millennium, possibly even earlier. Their civilization came to an end around 1750 B.C.
Sumer would have seemed old even to the Israelites, somewhat like
Roman civilization is to modern America. Important Sumerian cities

included Uruk, where *Gilgamesh* is set, and Ur, the city of the biblical patriarch Abraham. As for its technology, the Sumerians certainly could not be accused of reinventing the wheel, as they devised the very first one, as well as the sexagesimal (60-based) numerical system, which is the basis of our present-day time system.

In his commentary on Genesis, Old Testament scholar Derek Kidner observes a number of striking similarities between Sumerian and Hebrew. For instance, the term for Eden in Genesis 2:8 ("And the Lord God planted a garden in Eden") "seems to be related to the Sumerian term *edin(na)*," which means "plain or steppe" (62). And the word for "pitch," in Genesis 6:14 ("Make thee an ark of gopher wood; rooms shalt thou make in the ark, and shalt pitch it within and without with pitch") is *k-p-r*, or, when vocalized, *koper,* in Hebrew. It appears to be the Hebrew equivalent of the same term used in *Gilgamesh,* that is, *kupru* (97).

Further parallels between *Gilgamesh* and Genesis include the fact that both feature lists of men who enjoyed extraordinarily long lives. Granted, the longest-lived of Genesis's patriarchs, Methuselah, died at age 969, which is paltry compared to one Sumerian king, En-men-lu-Anna, who was on the throne for a staggering 43,200 years. Even so, both spans are superhuman. What is more, a flood disrupts both lines, and after the deluge, in both books, people live far shorter lives. And there may be further evidence of *Gilgamesh* influencing the Old Testament, not just in Genesis but also in the book of Ecclesiastes, which contains a number of verbal phrases and images that seem to parallel the Mesopotamian work.

For instance, the notion of life as vanity, especially as wind, is a common theme in Ecclesiastes and may find its origin in Gilgamesh's remark to his friend Enkidu, "Our days / are few in number, and whatever we achieve / is a puff of wind" (III, 93). So too, Gilgamesh's citation of a proverb, also spoken to Enkidu—"a three-ply rope is not easily broken" (V, 119)—could be reflected by Ecclesiastes 4:12, which reads, in the King James version, "And if one prevail against him, two shall withstand him; and a threefold cord is not quickly broken." Ecclesiastes was composed in the 1st millennium B.C. by either King Solomon or another educated person, so it is plausible that they would have had access to *Gilgamesh.* What is more, archaeologists have discovered a fragment of the *Epic* copied by an unknown scribe in northern Israel around the 14th century B.C. (Kaiser and Garrett 1027).

Kidner sums up the majority view, which is that "some version of the Babylonian stories, which were certainly copied and recopied centuries before Moses, must be the raw material of which Genesis is the finished product" (97). Of course, along with the many parallels, there are crucial differences; for instance, in *Gilgamesh*, the flood is sent, not because of wickedness, but on account of human over-population. In fact, one god, Ea, reveals the other gods' plans to destroy the world to Utnapishtim (a Noah-like character) so that Utnapishtim can construct a boat and save his family. Ea later berates the deity Enlil for sending the flood out of rashness: "You, the wisest and bravest of the gods, / how did it happen that you so recklessly / sent the Great Flood to destroy mankind?" (XI, 189). Ea also argues that not all humans were sinners and offers the intriguing notion that "[i]nstead of a flood, you should have sent / lions to decimate the human race, / or wolves, or a famine, or a deadly plague" (190). In addition, in *Gilgamesh*, the gods eat the sacrifice offered by Utnapishtim, the Noah figure, while in Genesis, Yahweh merely savors the fragrance of the meat offered by Noah (Alter 48).

Nevertheless, if Genesis is generally derivative of *Gilgamesh*, which in turn was inspired by *Atra-Hasis*, it would appear to place the biblical narrative at two removes from an actual flood/s. Thus, Genesis would seem to lack the kind of eyewitness quality that is the hallmark of true geomyths. On this view, the editor/s of Genesis would seem to be, in effect, appropriating the earlier story/s, and in the process making his own more literary than the original. For example, at least one verse in the Flood narrative, Genesis 7:11, is poetic and may thus constitute "a fragment from an old epic poem" (Alter 44). Indeed, although Hebraist Robert Alter disagrees with this view, he translates the verse poetically in a couplet: "All the well-springs of the great deep burst / and the casements of the heavens were opened."

Even so, all three tales are set in Mesopotamia, a Greek term that means "between the two rivers," and which refers to the land that is between the Tigris and Euphrates rivers. And each depicts a colossal flood, based, perhaps, on an actual, enormous regional deluge. In addition, both *Gilgamesh* and Genesis offer details worth considera-tion from a scientific point of view. Such items are relatively consistent in the various permutations of the narrative, suggesting that at least some of them are original. As noted in the introduction, while nu-merous non-essential facets may change over time in oral narratives, there is also striking continuity between tellings. Summing up, then, it is plausible that the deluge myths are showing us, however indirectly, something of what really happened.

For *Gilgamesh* and Genesis, two issues may be considered in geo-mythical terms: soil liquefaction and the Black Sea Deluge Hypothesis. Regarding the former, *Gilgamesh* has been studied by engineering geologist Ellis Krinitzsky, who argues that "*Gilgamesh* ... magnifies [the catastrophe] by having the flood begin with winds, lightning, and a shattering of the earth, or earthquake" (295). He contends, further, that both the epic as well as Genesis show signs of soil liquefaction, which is "an abrupt loss of strength in a cohesionless, water-saturated soil that results in its behaving like a liquid" (296). Soil liquefaction yields a kind of quicksand and is often produced by powerful earthquakes. The process can, among other things, cause water to "spout through [openings in the soil], carrying soil with it. These are like fountains of gushing water, and they continue to flow even after the earthquake shaking has stopped" (296). Krinitsky cites the Kobe (Japan) earthquake of 1995 as evidence of the phenomenon and argues that during the catastrophe, "water ... gushed from the ground ... to a height of 8 feet" (297). Such an event, he believes, could also have inspired the image of the "fountains of the great deep" opening up in Genesis 7:11, already noted. In addition, Krinitzsky cites passages from *Gilgamesh* that he believes "[represent] soil liquefaction" (295).

Dorothy Vitaliano also points out that Mesopotamia "is seismically unstable," and adds that "in the alluvial plains of great rivers water frequently spurts out in great fountains when the ground is compressed by earthquake stresses" (155). She remarks, further, that "such jets of subterranean water were observed in the New Madrid [Missouri] earthquakes of 1811-12" (155). In fact, one witness of the quakes, a surveyor named Louis Bringier, noted that "water ... rushed out in all quarters, bringing with it an enormous quantity of carbonized wood ... which was ejected to the height of from ten to fifteen feet, and fell in a black shower, mixed with ... sand" (qtd. in de Boer and Sanders "Earthquakes" 120).

As Krinitzsky explains, in *Gilgamesh*, an important proto-geological moment occurs in Book VI, when the Bull of Heaven is sent by the goddess Ishtar to punish Gilgamesh for rejecting her advances. Earlier in the narrative, Gilgamesh, who is king of Uruk, had gone to the Cedar Forest with his friend Enkidu to slay Humbaba, a monster who is the Forest's keeper. They return in triumph, having defeated Humbaba, and after Gilgamesh bathes and dresses in fresh clothing, the goddess Ishtar is smitten with his handsome appearance. She invites him to marry her, but he spurns her, citing her abandonment of other lovers in the past. Deeply insulted, Ishtar turns for help to her father, Anu, who reluctantly allows her to use the Bull of Heaven to kill Gilgamesh.

When the Bull descends to earth, it snorts and spits, and holes and chasms open up in the ground. In Stephen Mitchell's version, the narrator notes that "[w]hen the Bull snorted, the earth cracked open /

and a hundred warriors fell in and died" (137). The earth splits two more times, and the third time it does so, Enkidu, Gilgamesh's fellow warrior, falls in, at which point the Bull "spat / its slobber into his face" and "lifted / its tail and spewed dung all over him" (137). Hence, Krinitzsky argues that the fact that "the Bull [is] slavering or throwing spittle [in the face of Enkidu, Gilgamesh's companion] ... [could indicate] earthquake-induced soil liquefaction that caused a gushing of water with soil" (302).

He concedes that the Genesis account does not touch on earthquakes but notes that "the idea of both earthquakes and soil liquefaction may be embedded in the reference to the sudden bursting of water [in Genesis 7:11] from well-springs" (310). And Vitaliano follows Edward Suess's supposition that the image of the gushing springs "appears to be a later embellishment of the flood story," and wonders if this detail "originated from some observations of [other] waters spouting from the ground during an earthquake" (qtd. in Vitaliano 156).

The Black Sea Deluge Hypothesis

Of all the recent scientific theories related to the inundation myths, the Black Sea Deluge Hypothesis has perhaps drawn the most attention. It was first argued for by the oceanographer William Ryan et al. in a 1997 paper ("An Abrupt"), then followed by a popular 1999 book, co-authored by Ryan and William Pitman, entitled *Noah's Flood: The New Scientific Discoveries about the Event that Changed History*. The basic claim is that in the post-Late Glacial Maximum period (the last major ice age), which took place approximately 9,400 years ago, the Black Sea, once landlocked, became reconnected to the Mediterranean Sea as glaciers melted and seas rose. Waters surged from the Aegean Sea into the Dardanelles (a natural strait), then into the Sea of Marmara. From there, they shot through another natural strait, the Bosporus, and then broke through into the Black Sea. These incoming waters inundated a large number of people living on the sea's shore. Those who survived fled the area to the southeast, into Mesopotamia. They eventually became the ancestors of the Sumerians, who preserved the tale of the massive flood for generations (Montgomery 223) (Figure 2.2).

At present, the Hypothesis remains viable and, not surprisingly, controversial. Since Ryan's initial paper, other researchers have proposed less drastic scenarios. Aksu et al., for instance, argued in a 2002 study that there was no "catastrophic flooding but rather ... a slow establishment of two-way flow in the Bosporus and a time lag during which the fresher waters of the deep Black Sea were replaced by more

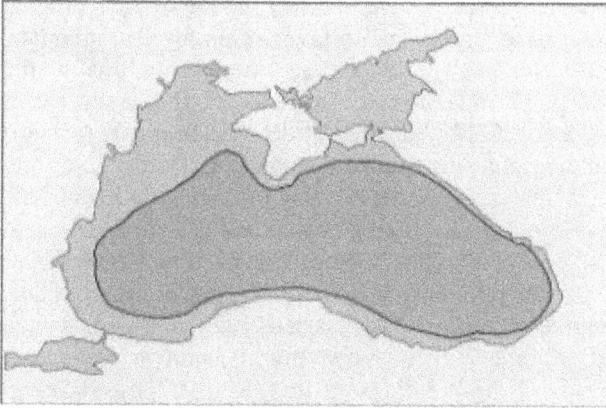

Figure 2.2 An illustration of the Black Sea Deluge Hypothesis. The smaller image represents the Black Sea prior to the alleged flooding, while the larger one is the Sea's present location. Wikimedia Commons.

saline inflow" (1). Another group, led by geophysicist Liviu Giosan, contended that during the period in question, the Black Sea was only 30 meters lower than its present height, not 80, as Ryan et al. claimed. Hence, while not ruling out a flood altogether, Giosan's team declared that "the sea level increase and the flooded area during the reconnection were significantly smaller than previously proposed" (1).

Since then, the pendulum has swung back. A 2017 study, led by Anastasia Yanchilina and co-authored with Ryan and other researchers, argues that geochronological, geochemical, and geophysical data show, among other things, that the "transgression [of the Black Sea by the Mediterranean's incoming waters] is likely to have been rapid rather than gradual ..., similar to phenomena observed during dam breakage" (28). Furthermore, the Black Sea shelf "was dry before submergence and the shoreline of the pre-boreal lake may [afterward] have regressed to beyond 120 [meters below sea level]" (14). In any event, given the cultural and scientific stakes of the Hypothesis, it seems safe to say that it will remain contested for some time.

One aspect of the theory, that the flood was regional rather than universal, might seem, at first, to conflict both with *Gilgamesh*, where Utnapishtim notes that from the ship's deck "[n]o land could be seen, just water on all sides" (XI, 187), and with Genesis 7:19–20: "And the waters prevailed so mightily upon the earth that *all the high mountains* under the whole heaven were covered; the waters *prevailed above the mountains, covering them fifteen cubits deep"* (my emphases). These and related biblical passages have provided young earth creationists with encouragement as they argue in favor of a universal inundation. Yet geoscientists have engaged these descriptions, both to refute the young earth claims and, in some cases, to reconcile the verses with the geological evidence. Space constraints do not permit us to marshal the many counterarguments against the young earth approach, but we can touch on a few that enable the Hypothesis to remain viable as a possible source of Genesis and *Gilgamesh.*

For instance, petrologist Lorence Collins argues against a common claim of the universalists, that is, that rocks on all continents have fossils trapped in them. This is because, as the argument goes, God destroyed all life on earth—Noah and his family excepted, of course. Collins responds by pointing out that, in fact, these rocks are interlayered with evaporite rock salt, gypsum, anhydrite, potash, and magnesium salts. Additionally, these salts are associated with red beds (shales) that contain mud cracks (38). The beds "have combined thicknesses on different continents of more than one kilometer." Their red hue stems from the fact that "they contain red hematite (iron oxide) which formed from magnetite grains that were oxidized while the muds were exposed to oxygen in open air" (39). The only thing that would cause mud cracks to form would be drying from the sun that causes "mud to shrink and form polygonal cracks" (39). These "evaporate mineral compounds ... are deposited in the correct chemical order predicted by the solubility of each kind of ion in these compounds and whose increasing concentrations during evaporation ... would cause them to precipitate in a predictable depositional sequence" as the waters diminished during multiple, smaller events, rather than a single massive occurrence (39).

Collins's point is that if there had been one universal flood, we would expect for "these evaporites to be at the top of the Noachian Flood deposits when the water supposedly receded, and the land dried out" (39). Instead, we see evaporites permeating the beds "in different levels in between older and younger fossiliferous 'Flood deposits'" (39). The only way to arrive at having the evaporites distributed throughout, at varying levels, would be to have normal flood patterns, that is,

> flooding, then drying to a dry earth, more flooding, more drying to a dry earth, *in repeated cycles that occur over and over again* ... [T]he kinds of evaporite deposits and red bed in many different levels ... could form only in local climates with desert drying conditions and could *not possibly have formed all at the same time.* (39; my emphases)

A related piece of evidence—one claimed by both sides—is the dense deposits of fossilized shells and on hills and mountain-tops, even on Mt. Everest, that are, in some cases, hundreds of miles inland. Church fathers such as St. Augustine seized on these deposits as proof of a global flood, yet Leonardo da Vinci correctly pointed out that shells and rocks typically are *not* carried by water but instead tend to sink, so he was skeptical about the claim of water—even strong floodwater—lifting shells to the tops of these peaks. Plus, building on Collins's argument about evaporites, the sheer density and layered quality of these shells argues against their being laid out in a one-time event. In fact, Mayor points out that "'shelly' limestone was a ubiquitous building material in antiquity," described by Pausanias as being "soft and extremely white, with seashells *all the way through it*" ("Fossil" 65; my emphasis). Mainstream scientists explain the phenomenon of shells on hills and mountain-tops by positing that the remains of organic creatures, once submerged and then fossilized, were subsequently lifted up, not by surging waters but rather by plate tectonics that caused mountains to rise from valleys.

As for the biblical and Gilgameshic claims that "all the earth" was flooded, Montgomery notes that in the former case, translation could be an issue, as the Hebrew terms for earth (*eretz* or *adamah*) can also be rendered as "land" or "country." And saying "all the *land* was covered"—instead of the entire planet—feels far less universal. Indeed, geologist Carol Hill insists that "[i]n no way can the term 'earth' be taken to mean the planet Earth, as in Noah's time and place, people ... had no concept of Earth as a planet and thus had no word for it" (171).

In addition, Collins puts forth a striking hypothesis that the biblical references to "all the earth" being flooded could have sprung from an optical illusion. That is, if a Noah or Utnapishtim figure stood on top of an ark or large boat in the water, one that extended eight meters or so above the water, "given the earth's roundness, he would not be able to see the tops of any hills as high as 15 meters from as little as 24 km away across flood plains covered with water, because the curvature of the earth prevents it" (41). Collins observes that "[m]ost hills in this region [that is, the watershed of the Euphrates and Tigris rivers] that are as much as 15 meters high are more than 95 km away from the river levees." In other words, "the survivors of the Flood could see *only water in all directions* while they were floating down the Tigris River and over the flood plains" (40; my emphasis). Hence, it is quite possible that they believed they were seeing the whole planet covered with water, even if they were not.

Earthquake and Tsunami Myths

Earthquakes are often the cause of tsunamis; hence legends about both events frequently go together. Such is the case with the Atlantis narrative, perhaps the most famous myth of all time. Atlantis was said to be an island-state that existed long ago. It boasted advanced technology and was a kind of utopia, yet it was eventually destroyed by a huge tsunami. The story is first set forth in Plato's dialogues *Timaeus* and *Critias*, which tell of how Atlantis's destruction by the enormous breaker was preceded by strong quakes.

In terms of its universality, the legend cannot be surpassed: nearly every continent and landmass has been identified at one time or another as the mythical site. Atlantis has fired the imagination of writers and artists for centuries; notable works indebted to the legend include Thomas More's *Utopia*, Francis Bacon's *The New Atlantis*, and J.R.R. Tolkien's *The Silmarillion*. It has also spawned colorful cultural theories: the Basque nation, for instance, traces its ancestry to the nation of Atlantis, since until recently, the Basque language (Euskera) had no known connections with any presently spoken languages. The Nazis, moreover, claimed a link to the continent, regarding it as populated by an Aryan race.

Hence, it would seem logical for a study of geomythology to engage the legend. Its charm and popularity notwithstanding, however, it is almost certainly a rare example of a myth that is almost completely fabricated, with little or no connection to a real place. Vitaliano included it in her survey of possible geotales, but we have no evidence that Plato himself actually believed it. Nor did anyone else from antiquity, as far as we know. Even so, Atlantis continues to exert a strong cultural influence, and new candidates for it are constantly forthcoming.

One of the more recent ones, which has the distinction of being a real site, is Doggerland, the presently submerged landmass between the United Kingdom and Europe (Figure 2.3). It was once populated by humans, up until what journalist Richard Webb calls, wittily if inaccurately, "Brexit: 10,000 years B.C." He is referring to the results of the Storegga Slides, which occurred off of Norway's coast about 8,000 years ago, and which constituted some of the largest landslides ever, with an astonishing total of about 180 miles of coastal shelf suddenly breaking off (Bondevik et al. 289). These Slides created a colossal tsunami, which quickly submerged Doggerland. However, we have few records of any cultural artifacts from Doggerland, so at present, it holds little value from a geomythical perspective.

On the other hand, turning to East Asian literature, we have what is sometimes called the "Indian Atlantis," that is, Dwarka, a fabled city

Figure 2.3 Map of Doggerland, situated between the United Kingdom, continental Europe, and Norway.

made of precious stones and boasting 900,000 palaces. It was founded by the god Krishna, as recounted in the venerable Indian epic *Mahābhārata*, or "Great War." In the epic's sixteenth book, Dwarka is deluged by tremendous waves and eventually disappears, seemingly without a trace. Yet in 1963, marine archaeologist Shikaripura Rao made a stunning discovery: he and his team found extensive ruins in the waters off Gujarat (western India), near the alleged site of the ancient city (Rao 51–59).

Commenting on the find, Rao stated that "[w]e can't rule out the possibility of a tsunami drowning ancient Dwarka as the town was rapidly inundated by some sea activity," though he concedes that texts that supplement the *Mahābhārata,* including the *Bhagavad gita,* suggest that the flooding actually took seven days. More recently, civil engineer R. N. Iyengar and B.P. Radhakrishna have surveyed the geological history of the western Gujarat region. While they note that "the postulated position of [Dwarka] as reviewed in the Sanskrit text appears to conform with the broad geological history of the region," they contend that the city was far inland, near Delhi, and is not the site discovered by Rao (285). Their call for further study of the questions surrounding this fabled metropolis makes good sense. One possible consideration is the cultural effects of the region's seismic activity, seen in events like the 2001 Gujarat quake, which measured 7.7 on the Richter scale.

Among western quake-based narratives, the Trojan War stands out. The alleged site of Troy, located in modern-day western Turkey, has been frequently excavated over the last two centuries by researchers following clues from Homer's *Iliad.* Multiple layers of the city have emerged, one of which, at least, was probably destroyed by an earthquake (Cline 105). This find has potential geomythical resonances. Geophysicist Amos Nur notes that the sea-god Poseidon, who favors the Greeks against the Trojans in the War, was known as the "god of earthquakes," and in book XX, he causes a powerful world-wide quake, one that shakes springs, ships, mountain-peaks, and most importantly, "the walls of Troy" (XX, 72).

We do not know what caused the city's destruction, along with other settlements in the region, around 1200 B.C. One common explanation has been an incursion/s by the so-called Sea Peoples. However, the precise identity of these alleged invaders has never been ascertained, and as Nur notes, "all the likely suspects seem to have been otherwise engaged at the time, either defending their own strongholds or struggling to preserve their own declining social structures" (17–18). He observes that the area lies on the North Anatolian Fault, which runs from northern Turkey through Greece (Nur 236), and proposes that a "swarm" of earthquakes in the region felled the cities. While it is not possible to prove that such a swarm occurred, the high seismicity of the area, along with the frequent occurrence of quakes during modern times, makes it plausible. Regarding the latter, for instance, a powerful tremor hit western Turkey in 1912, and the archaeological site of Troy was affected (238).

Another mythic narrative from the classical tradition which appears to be linked with seismic activity and which may pre-date the Troy legend is the stunning death of Amphiaraus, the fabled seer-king of

Greece. As a member of the so-called Seven Against Thebes, he assisted Polyneices's doomed attempt to regain the throne of Thebes from Polyneices's brother Eteocles. Earlier, following the death of their father, Oedipus (notorious for killing his father and marrying his mother), the brothers had agreed to share the throne, exchanging the rulership each year with one another. But when Eteocles refused to step down after his first year, Polyneices summoned allies, including Amphiaraus, from the surrounding kingdoms to help him assert his rights. This septet assailed the Theban gates but was repelled and pursued by the defenders. Amphiaraus was chased by Periclymenus, a son of Poseidon. As he fled, he drove his chariot along the river Ismenus, with Periclymenus in hot pursuit. The latter was just about to hurl his spear at the fugitive when the earth opened up and swallowed Amphiaraus, along with his charioteer and four-horse team.

As horrific as such a death might appear to modern readers, its actual effect, strangely, was to preserve Amphiaraus's body whole as he made his way to the underworld. Indeed, in the Roman poet Statius's version (*The Thebaid*), the narrator notes that "Apollo sadly sheds a vain lustre on his servant," and intends, further, that "no mortal weapon should have power to harm [Amphiaraus], but that he should go to Dis *sacred and venerable in death*" (6.688 ff.; my emphasis). Zeus was known for looking favorably on seers and protecting them to the extent that he could.

Cindy Clendenon, a researcher in the field of hydromythology, has studied this narrative and others from the period in terms of karstic landscapes. These are "regions underlain by caves in limestone bedrock," and often feature sinkholes created when the caves buckle (Marshak G-12). Taking the Thebes narrative as containing at least a grain of truth, she argues that Amphiaraus met his doom because of "an earthquake-induced ground rupture or possibly an earthquake-induced roof collapse of a large cavern or sinkhole" (Clendenon 330). A sinkhole, she explains, is "a closed, pit-like depression in the land surface that forms when underlying rock material is removed primarily by dissolution and transport, creating a void into which the cover material slumps, sinks, or collapses," and adds that "a sinkhole may appear either gradually or suddenly" (266). Clendenon also notes that such subsidence can be brought on by floods, heavy rain, or quakes. She believes that "[in the] Seven Against Thebes battle ... a series of precursor earthquakes and perhaps the main earthquake itself probably triggered a collapse that otherwise was eminent [sic]" (267).

Modern examples of large sinkholes include Cedar Sink in Mammoth Caves National Park (Kentucky, USA), which is 300 feet deep, and one in the Tampa, Florida area that is about 60 feet deep. The latter hole has achieved a kind of notoriety and, we might say, constitutes a gruesome, modern-day counterpart to Amphiaraus's. On February 28, 2013, in a Tampa suburb, 36-year-old Jeff Bush was lying on his bed in his home as he and his family settled down for the evening. Minutes later, there was a loud noise, and a large sinkhole suddenly yawned directly underneath the one-story house. Bush found himself plunging through his bedroom floor, along with his bed, television, and dresser. His brother Jeremy rushed to help him, but Bush was unable to extricate himself from the pit, which eventually swelled to its present depth. After search-and-rescue teams frantically tried to save Bush, they finally had to give up. His body has never been recovered, and the house was later demolished ("Florida Man") (Figure 3.1).

Earthquakes can cause sinkholes to form. In Statius's account, he includes a description of a strong tremor occurring just before the cavity opens: "And now little by little the earth began to shudder to its rending, and the surface to rock, and the dust to rise in thicker clouds, already an infernal bellowing fills the plain." Both Amphiaraus and Periclymenus interpret the sound as nearby battle noises, but Clendenon suggests that it was, in fact, the roar of a quake. In addition, according to Statius, the river itself "flees with all his banks exposed to view." Clendenon speculates that, at this point, "the [karstic] riverbed either subsided or shifted laterally, or both" (340–41). She also cites possible other influences that precipitated the sinkhole's formation, including "torrential flooding caused by seasonal spring rains and snowmelt, ice-breaking and snow-shifting on the surrounding mountains" (33). Furthermore, the death of Amphiaraus is preceded by a curious fact, namely, that "already"—that is, prior to the tremor—"his horses ... fear the ground" (7.688). As Clendenon explains, "many animals display unusual behavior just prior to an earthquake" (340). In sum, while the account of Amphiaraus's shocking death is ancient, it may reflect the eye- and ear-witnesses of an actual event.

Tsunamis in Indigenous Tales

Indigenous narratives sometimes seem to be inspired by tsunamis, along with related phenomena. Nunn et al. have studied the disappearance of various South Sea islands, including Teonimanu, formerly part of the Solomon Islands, northeast of Australia. They consulted with elders, including one who shared an account that had been handed down to him. It concerned a man named Rapuanate, who lived on Ali'ite, a nearby island, and who obtained a wife from the island of Teonimanu.

Later, when he was away, her brother came and returned her to Ali'ite. After trying unsuccessfully to win her back, Rapuanate hired a witch to hex Teonimanu. She gave him three taro seedlings known for having edible roots. He was directed to plant two on Teonimanu, and the third on his own island. When his own seedling would begin sprouting leaves, he was told, that would be the sign that Teonimanu was on the verge of sinking. The spell worked: not long after he completed the planting, the sea rose and inundated Teonimanu. Some inhabitants survived on rafts; others climbed coconut and banana trees but perished when waves started crashing into the island (Nunn et al. 42–43).

Teonimanu appears to have been present during the 1586 explora-tion of the area by Spanish navigator Álvaro de Mendaña y Neira but was gone by the time James Cook was investigating the neighboring island of Vanuatu about 200 years later (Nunn et al. 43). Based on the oral narrative alone, it could appear that a tsunami swallowed the island, yet this is a geological impossibility. Nunn and his team identify it as one of several "bedrock islands" in the region and contend that, as such, "[the islands] could not have disappeared simply by wave im-pact" (44). Instead, waves, combined with other factors, such as the collapsing of the side or sides of the islands, could have caused the island to vanish. Earthquakes might have been an influence, too, given that this region is close to "convergent plate boundaries" (45). Subsidence and uplift from quakes are prevalent in the area, making it "uncommonly unstable" (45). And volcanic collapse is also likely, given that the area is part of a volcanically active arc.

A somewhat similar narrative comes from the Maori nation. It was recorded by Albert Grace, a writer and teacher, in 1907 and is titled "The Rival Wizards." The story was told to Grace by Karept Te Whetu, an elder in the Ngati Koata nation (King et al. 907). It con-cerns a contest between one "wizard," Te Pou, and another named Titipa. After catching a mess of fish, Titipa boasted of his haul, yet Te Pou insisted that he, not Titipa, be awarded the choicest fish from the catch. When Titipa refused his demand, Te Pou exercised his powers, summoning three massive waves, and while Te Pou and the bystanders quickly ran to high ground, Titipa was left alone on the beach. As the first wave receded, it began sucking Titipa and the fish out to sea. By the time the second and third ones crashed ashore, the beach was empty (King et al. 908).

This narrative, along with similar ones, has been used by scientists to understand the effects of tsunamis, including the experiences of those caught by the waves. Such stories often prove invaluable since they "can provide independent sources of information [that] complement geological and archaeological knowledge" about cataclysmic episodes (King et al. 909). One reason for this is that many such tales, including "The Rival Wizards," supplement the "limited time frame of the historical record" (King et al. 909), which, of course, only goes back as far as written records have been kept. Commenting on the tale, geologist David Bressan notes that its use of specific names suggests that it is based on the experience of an actual tsunami, one that may have hit New Zealand's South Island around the 1400s or so (par. 5). As a result of studying these narratives, scientists can refine the historical record of areas where tsunamis may occur again and can improve hazard maps for future catastrophes (par. 6). We will say more about this in chapter 4. First, however, we will sharpen our focus by turning from universal geomyths to those linked with specific areas or regions.

3 Regional Geomyths

Griffins and Dinosaurs

How does it feel to be buried alive in a sandstorm? It may have happened to a Persian army, some 50,000 strong, in the Sahara Desert. In or around 525 B.C., these troops had been dispatched by the Persian king Cambyses II, son of Cyrus. Cambyses was nettled by a renegade outpost of priests serving in the temple of Amun, Egypt, who refused to acknowledge his sovereignty. According to the ancient historian Herodotus (484–25 B.C.), the soldiers never reached Amun; instead, they were smothered to death when taking their lunch by a "southerly wind of extreme violence" (Burn 214).

Most historians discount the story as pure fiction or as wild exaggeration, nor is it clear that sandstorms are fatal to humans, though they can certainly impede our breathing and compromise our sense of direction. On the other hand, there is a type of animal killed by dust-storms: the dinosaur *Protoceratops*, whose skeletons, often completely articulated and standing upright, are found in the Gobi Desert, which covers parts of northern China and southern Mongolia (Figure 3.1). From prehistory till now, this area has been one of the world's largest producers of dust. Even millions of years ago, storms here could become so intense that dinosaurs caught outside in them were essentially paralyzed, frozen in place, until they died. Some of these skeletons fossilized, and ages hence were discovered by human travelers. They appear to have inspired tales of griffins.

If there is a geomythology icon, a single example that sums up or symbolizes the geomythical enterprise, we could do worse than select the griffin, a mythical composite creature with an eagle's head and wings combined with a lion's body (Figure 3.2). The griffin has seized the imagination of writers from Aeschylus through Dante to contemporary fantasists such as J.K. Rowling and Rick Riordan. It also provides a starting point for this chapter since, as noted, in their

Figure 3.1 *Protoceratops* skeleton, Royal Ontario Museum. Photo by Andrew Plumb. Wikimedia Commons.

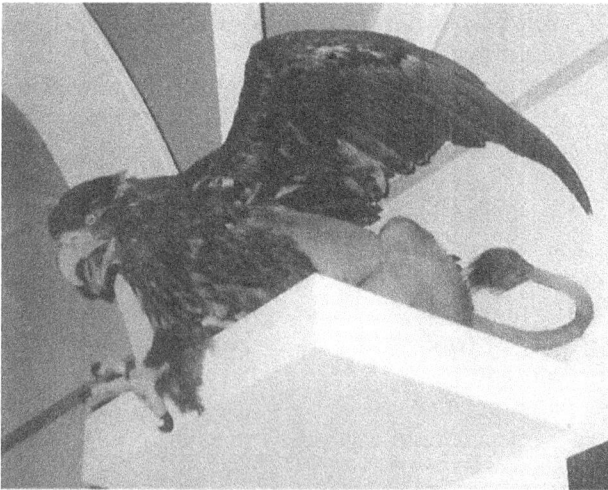

Figure 3.2 Stuffed (hoax) gryphon, Zoological Museum, Copenhagen, Denmark. Photo by FunkMonk. Wikimedia Commons.

origins, griffin myths were regionally based, closely connected with the desolate lands of central Asia. Griffin tales appear to have been invented and disseminated by an indigenous people-group known as the Saka-Scythians, a pre-literate culture, before being committed to writing by Herodotus and other Greek authors.

Adrienne Mayor has detailed possible ways the Scythians, who roamed the territory of Central Asia from the Black Sea to Inner Mongolia, could have envisioned the reality of griffins. In their travels, they encountered *Protoceratops* remains, or at least heard of them, and then creatively miscategorized them. While the griffin-*Protoceratops* link cannot be proved, as a supposition, Mayor's thesis has been endorsed by many paleontologists. Her absorbing account of this decade-long search for the griffin's folkloric origins is told in *The First Fossil-Hunters* (15–53). We will review some of her main points. Yet again, as with all geomyths, caution is in order since the griffin narratives could have arisen independently, with the finding of dinosaur bones merely "confirming" invented tales. Or, the bones could have been discovered first, followed by the tales.

The word "griffin" stems from the Greek term "gryps," which means "hooked," as in a beak; that term is related to the Persian *giriften*, that is, "to grip or seize" (Mayor, "First," 23). Griffins are first mentioned by the Greek writer Aristeas, who lived around 700 B.C., in his nearly nonextant epic poem, the *Arimaspeia*. (Two short excerpts from it appear in the works of the writers Longinus and John Tzetzes.) Aristeas was a semi-mythical figure, allegedly capable of self-resuscitation and time travel. There are two accounts of him dying and then appearing later, years hence in one instance, centuries in another; in the latter case, he took on the form of a raven. He wrote about his travels, and Herodotus cites some of these, including Aristeas's references both to the griffins and to the Arimaspeans, a one-eyed race of humans supposedly living in the same area (Burn 276). Aristeas claims to have heard these tales when he visited the Saka-Scythians around 675 B.C.

The area he explored is, as it were, a "four corners" region geographically, one that, as Mayor has it, "straddles present-day northwestern Mongolia, northwestern China, southern Siberia, and southeastern Kazakhstan" (26–27). And Mayor points out that "Greek and Roman trade with … [these] nomads flourished in this region from Aristeas's day to about A.D. 300 – exactly the period during which griffins were most prominently featured in Greco-Roman art and literature" (27).

Her search was motivated by the fact that while griffins are purely legendary, various details about their appearance and habitat seemed to point to real source/s. As she notes, unlike other hybrids of Greek legends, such as Pegasus, the Minotaur, and centaurs, "the griffin played no role in Greek mythology." Rather, it appears in Greek natural histories, leading her to surmise that it was "a creature of folklore grounded in naturalistic details" (16).

Mayor was also aware that other mythical creatures such as the Cyclopes and dragons might be partly based on the misidentification of actual remains. In her research, she learned that German physicist George Erman (1806–77) had had a similar intuition about griffins and, in fact, alleged that griffin stories were evoked by the exposed bones of "Ice Age rhinos and mammoths" (19). Erman was later castigated for only interviewing, in the course of his research, "Siberian informants living some 2,000 miles ... northwest of the origin [sites] of the griffin tale" (Mayor, "First" 21). Additionally, rhino and elephant skulls lack beaks, the "essential hallmark of griffins" (21). Still, he was on the right track, and as Mayor studied the problem, it became clear to her that "all the descriptions [of griffins] between 700 B.C. and A.D. 400 pointed to a specific homeland for griffins: the desolate wastes of Central Asia." Indeed, this area is so isolated that, amusingly, "the designers of atlases typically stitch page binding directly over [it] ... obliterating that map's topography as surely as any sandstorm" (22).

It is true, Mayor admits, that "strange creatures combining the features of birds and mammals had appeared earlier, in Near Eastern art, as early as 3000 B.C." She also concedes that "peacock-headed griffins can be seen in Mycenean art of the Greek Bronze Age (ca. 1200 B.C.)" (23, 25). We may also cite what could be called a "reverse" griffin in *Gilgamesh*: in the poem's seventh chapter, Enkidu, Gilgamesh's close friend, claims that he had a nightmare in which he saw a figure with a lion's head and paws, and an eagle's talons and wings (*Gilgamesh* 142). Again, though, unlike the artistic depictions, the griffin stories in the Greek authors are the first written ones, and assume that the creature *actually existed*; furthermore, the details they supply about its origins remain consistent.

For instance, all the sources, as mentioned, locate them in the same area of the world. Moreover, the creatures are often associated with gold, and in fact, are depicted as ferocious guardians of such treasure. Another telling detail, one that, like others, "remained consistent over a millennium," is that "they had four legs but also a beak" (Mayor, "First" 34). Modern paleontological research lines up with these claims. For instance, in the 1920s, central Asia was found to be a bonanza for bone-hunters, to the point that, in the words of one explorer, the very ground seemed "paved" with bones (40). Among their finds: four-legged, hook-nosed skeletons of the *Protoceratops* (Figure 3.1). Mayor notes that paleontologist Peter Dodson describes such remains as some of "the most ubiquitous ... in the Gobi" (43). With these clues in mind, Mayor studied bone discoveries in the region. She also reached out to two paleontologists who knew the area, and she floated the hypothesis of the griffin legends arising here. Mayor was gratified when "they agreed that ancient nomads certainly would have observed constantly emerging, fully articulated skeletons of beaked dinosaurs." Further evidence came to light, such as the fact that "the protoceratopsids were about the size of wolves or lions, and [that] they resembled large, flightless, four-legged raptors." Again, this description lines up with the combination of lion and eagle traits seen in griffins. In addition, the fossil beds of these dinosaurs are quite close to the area of the region's many gold deposits, which fact could have "led to the notion that [the griffins] 'guarded' [it]" (43). Adding up the data, the mystery appeared to be solved, or at least plausibly explained: griffin stories were certainly influenced by, and conceivably inspired by, the fossils.

In addition to the sheer fun of the detective work involved, Mayor's hypothesis is significant for at least two other reasons. First: griffins, with their beaks, wings, and feathers, anticipate one of paleontology's major finds in the last two decades, that certain dinosaurs were quite bird-like; some were even feathered (45). Furthermore, birds today are regarded as dinosaurs and, in fact, are known as "avian dinosaurs." According to geologist Kenneth Lacovara, just like their ancestors, birds possess strong legs and a bone structure that allows for vigorous, forward motion. Indeed, he remarks, "once your mind is tuned for the requisite ready-for-action dinosaur anatomy ... you'll start to notice the inner dinosaur in every bird, from a penguin to a pigeon" (25).

Second, as we have seen, griffin tales were created by indigenes: the Saka-Scythians. While the Greeks set the fables down in writing, the narratives originated with the Scythians, who were nomadic, prospected for gold, and sported tattoos. They also valued natural objects such as shells from the *Gryphaea* family, which they placed into family graves (Mayor, "First" 166). (It would be tempting to see an etymological connection between *Gryphaea*-griffin, but in fact, the former term refers to a type of extinct oyster.) Yet once more, then, geomythology shows how seemingly primitive people inadvertently anticipated important scientific discoveries.

Gold-mining Ants

Griffins are not the only mythological creatures associated with gold, aside from dragons. There is a third whose links with the precious metal may be rather surprising: ants. These insects are regarded in certain myths as not only protecting but, more startlingly, *mining* gold. As with griffins, Herodotus is a crucial source. In fact, it is stories like these that earned him the dubious title of "The Father of Lies" in the classical world. Yet geomythology may serve to exonerate him somewhat.

In some ways, the nickname was never quite fair. For instance, Burn points out that Herodotus often admits to his own skepticism about certain claims even as he shares them with his readers. Herodotus presents the account of the Arimaspeans in this questioning manner (250). At other times he touches on the truth without fully realizing it, such as when he mentions the theory, now scientifically established, that the annual Nile flood was precipitated by snowmelt in the Ethiopian mountains (29–30). Furthermore, Mayor observes that Herodotus's allegations about the region of the Saka-Scythians are increasingly confirmed by archaeology, so that he is "beginning to be appreciated as a faithful recorder of historical reality as well as popular beliefs" ("First" 30).

Hence, as far-fetched as Herodotus's account of gold-mining ants may seem, it contains a morsel of truth—a nugget, we might say. Regarding the (East Asian) Indian tribes, Herodotus notes that "in this region ... there is a sandy desert. There is found ... a kind of ant of great size—bigger than a fox, though not so big as a dog" (Burn 246). Furthermore, he notes, "these creatures as they burrow ... throw up the sand in heaps, just as our own ants throw up the earth, and they are very like ours in shape. The sand has a rich content of gold, and this it is that the Indians are after when they make their expeditions into the desert" (246). Herodotus points out that they gather the metal during the hottest part of the day when the ants are underground (247). The Indians fill their bags with sand and exit as quickly as possible, "for the ants... smell them and at once give chase; nothing in the world can touch these ants for speed, so not one of the Indians would get home alive, if they did not make sure of a good start while the ants were mustering their forces" (247).

Burn dismisses the narrative as "a remarkably tall story" (29), yet here too the ancient writer has been at least partly vindicated. Starting in the early 1980s, ethnologist Michel Peissel began studying these references in the *Histories* while simultaneously applying for permits to explore the area in question near the border of Kashmir and India. (This site is a geopolitical hotspot; India and Pakistan have fought over Kashmir for centuries.) He finally succeeded and discovered the animal that may have inspired the tale.

Thankfully, at least from a human perspective, the size of Herodotus's ants is greatly embellished. The largest ants known today are bullet and bull ants. The former type is found in Brazil, and their sting reportedly feels like a gunshot (hence the name), while the latter is native to Australia. Both species can reach two inches in length: an impressive size, but nowhere approaching canine dimensions. However, there *is* one animal that is bigger than a fox, yet smaller than a dog, which lives in the area in question, and most importantly, which seems to "mine" gold, not consciously, but by flipping sand into the air when it is digging, then guarding it fiercely. This is the Himalayan marmot, which tends to be large and territorial, and which has razor-sharp teeth.

The ant-marmot link was the essence of Peissel's discovery, and as he recounted in an interview, and in a subsequent book (*The Ants' Gold*), it was confirmed for him when he heard "the startling news that [local villagers] used to collect the earth from the marmot burrows because it contained much gold dust" (qtd. in Simons). He also speculates that Herodotus may have been confused by the fact that in Persian, the word "marmot" is equivalent to the phrase "mountain ant." There is no clear evidence that Herodotus knew Persian, though the Persians invaded his hometown of Halicarnassus in 480 B.C. Just possibly, Herodotus had a smattering of the language, enough to muddle him on this point.

The historian's essential trustworthiness may be strengthened as well by the fact that certain animals and insects, including not just marmots and ants, but termites and even earthworms, "mine" gold. Of course, this is not a conscious action; the insects apparently select the gold because it is soft and thus relatively easy to bite with their mandibles. In fact, insects have been helpful for scientists and other researchers who are trying to access bedrock in areas covered with relatively deep regolith, which is the loose soil that lies atop bedrock. Often this soil blows in from other locations, so sampling it tells the scientists little about the underlying rock. This is where the insects come into play, as they burrow beneath the topsoil, then reemerge with material from below it. Their "mining" action is known as bioturbation, which is the movement of loose soil by animals and insects. In building their nests and mounds, they take gold fragments, along with other related minerals, such as kimberlite (an igneous rock that sometimes houses diamonds), copper, nickel, and turquoise.

In some cases, ants even bring up microfossils from underground areas that are difficult for humans to access. Regarding this fossil "hunting" by the ants, geologist Jim Davis, writing for the Utah Geological Survey, notes that one local harvester ant mound contained some 1,100 bones from nine mammal species (par. 12). He also points out that paleontologists have learned to use ants to collect bones. The so-called "ant hill method ... can increase bone collection rates by more than 40-fold." Not only that, but this method can also help researchers gain more precise measurements about subterranean bone-beds. An Upper Cretaceous bed was studied in just this way—one ant bed alone, he notes, held "more than 327 fossil teeth" (par. 14). However, such research had to be carried out with caution since the harvester ant venom is the most toxic in the world.

Mayor tells the story of John Bell Hatcher, a paleontologist who perfected this method while bone-hunting in the 1880s in the western U.S. He would sift through piles of sand from the mounds and claimed, "I frequently secured from 200 to 300 teeth and jaws from one ant hill" (qtd. in Mayor, "Fossil" 218). Hatcher also had the ingenuity to transport both sand and ants to various sites where he had discovered Cretaceous bones and then return after a time. By then, the insects would have built up a "collection" of bones that he would promptly harvest. He even took to crating up entire hills, then mailing them cross country to the eminent paleontologist O.C. Marsh at Yale University (in New Haven, Connecticut) for analysis (218-19).

Crater Legends and Geomythology

Another group of regional, "earth-based" geomyths are legends about meteors and asteroids and the impact craters they leave on our planet's surface. It might seem inaccurate to categorize these as regional since meteorites are a global phenomenon: a staggering 25 million of them enter our atmosphere daily. Thankfully, nearly all of these particles quickly burn up, though on average, about 17 still manage to hit the Earth every day (Lovett, "Earth"). In addition, craters have been discovered on or under every continent, including Antarctica.

Nevertheless, certain meteorite events are closely linked with specific regions; in fact, meteorites are generally named for the area in which they were found. The Aborigines have legends about them in their myths, some suggesting that certain of these events—even ones occurring thousands of years ago, incredibly—were witnessed, not merely inferred after the fact by visitors to the impact craters. Similarly, central Italy may have a large crater that appears to chime with a local legend about "statues" falling from the sky; the legend was preserved and passed down by an ethnic group known as the *superaequum*. And the well-known Tunguska event of 1908 was probably caused by an asteroid that exploded in the air on June 30, about 5 kilometers above eastern Siberia. It was so powerful it had the energy of a "10 to 30 megaton explosion," which is equivalent, as Kimberly

Smith notes, to "the blast energy of the 1980 Mt. St. Helens eruption" (par. 13). Though it merely grazed the Earth, it still managed to destroy 500,000 acres of forest (uninhabited, for the most part) and created a shock wave that was felt around the world (Smith par. 4). Many of the downed trees are there to this day.

Astronomer Duane Hamacher has been an important figure in the study of Aboriginal meteor stories. His research has focused on sites in the Henbury Meteorites Conservation Reserve, located about 145 km south of Alice Springs, in the heart of Australia. The craters here seem to have been formed about 5,000 years ago, probably by a meteor or asteroid that broke up in its descent, creating the main impact site as well as smaller depressions near it. For decades, however, they were not recognized by western scientists as impact sites. In fact, in 1899, Walter Parke, who at the time owned the land on which the Reserve is presently located, wrote to an anthropologist named Frank Gillen with a theory that the impressions were made by human agency (Zielinski par. 6).

Only later, in 1931, when iron slugs were discovered in the area did researchers realize what the hollows were. (Asteroids tend to be rich in this metal.) Yet, in a sense, the Aborigines had anticipated this finding by centuries, possibly even millennia. We know this because a (white) visitor to Henbury, who came in both 1921 and 1934, was guided by an Aboriginal (a member of the Luritja tribe) who refused to approach the craters. His reluctance stemmed from the fact that "it was a place where a fire 'debil debil' [devil] came out of the sky and killed everything in the vicinity." The guide also shared that he and his people did not even use water that collected in the depressions for fear that the fire devil would "fill them with a piece of iron." And he claimed that his grandfather "saw the fire devil, and [insisted that] it came from the sun" (Hamacher 3).

The images of burning fiends plunging from the sky and exploding with results fatal to all in the vicinity are astonishing and strongly suggest that the Aborigines recognized—in their own terms—the cosmic source of the Henbury craters. Hamacher, in addition, notes other Aboriginal groups living north of Henbury, including the Kaitish and Warramunga, who have similar traditions about fiery "debil-debils" descending from the heavens. While he touches on the possibility of "cultural contamination," that is, of western scientists planting the idea of falling meteors in the minds of Aboriginal hearers, Hamacher suspects that "the traditions ... were *pre*-colonial" (3; my emphasis). He then concludes that "the current evidence indicates that Aboriginal people *witnessed the event*, recorded the incident in oral tradition, and those traditions remained intact through the 1930s"

(3; my emphasis). This is a stunning claim, but one that seems plausible, given both the antiquity of the Aboriginal oral tradition, as well as the fact that, again, the source of the craters was not identified scientifically until the 1930s, well after the Aboriginal stories were formed.

Regarding the Italian episode about falling statues, in their 2003 study, Santilli et al. argue that in or around the 4th century A.D., in the central Italian region of Abruzzo, a meteorite exploded above the earth, somewhat like the Tunguska event. In fact, the team noted the similarities between the episodes: both consisted of meteors blowing up mid-air, though only the Abruzzo burst left what seems like craters. Moreover, it could have generated a shock wave, similar to the one at Tunguska, as well as a strong local earthquake (316). The study describes its likely appearance as "an approaching star turning into a bright fireball passing the atmosphere with … sonic booms" (316). Regarding the area in question, it features an oval-shaped depression on the ground measuring about 115 meters × 140 meters (or, 377 feet × 460 feet) approximately 53 meters (174 feet) deep on average (Torrese et al. 34). Close by are smaller depressions, a potential geological signature that led Santilli and his team to posit the breakage of the meteor above ground (313).

One part of their article seized the attention of the international media, namely, their suggestion that this event could have been witnessed by emperor Constantine. In 312 A.D., Constantine allegedly saw some kind of heavenly sign that spurred him on to a decisive victory against his rival Maxentius, thereby giving him complete control of the Roman empire. We will return to this claim shortly. First, however, it should be noted that the main thesis has received a fair amount of pushback from other geoscientists. For instance, a 2004 paper observes that the area in question has large chunks of limestone within it, and these would almost certainly be shattered by a meteor or asteroid's impact. There are also dating anomalies registered by the original team, with the main crater supposedly being carbon-dated to the 4th or 5th century A.D., but another pit, by contrast, dated to the 3rd millennium B.C. (Schneider par. 8). One alternate explanation is that the depression is not an impact site but rather an old reservoir dug for watering sheep and cattle. Advocates of this theory point out that the area was long known for wool production from the 12th to the 16th centuries (par. 10).

Yet, a 2019 paper by Torrese et al. strengthens the original claim that the hollow was created by an impact site. It considers other explanations, including water holes and mud volcanoes, only to rule them out. They point out that "the structure is too deep to have been dug out by humans," and note that it displays "the deep-seated overturning of strata" that would result from a powerful, non-human impact (Torrese et al. 38). They also state that "slow excavation by machinery or man-power would not reach these depths [50+ meters] before the walls would begin caving in due to the weight of the surrounding plain material" (36). Regarding the mud volcano theory, the researchers point out that the crater "lacks the downward continuation typical for the underground removal of material during karst development or the upwards transport of material from a deep-seated vent" (12). Still, they concede that the evidence is not definitive and allow, for instance, that the lack of "shock-metamorphic and/or geochemical evidence of impact" leaves non-impact possibilities open (38).

This article also revisits the allegation that Constantine could have witnessed the cosmic event (27, 28). Small wonder: the claim, if proven, could make this one of the most influential meteors in western history. Not only would the Abruzzo meteor have inspired Constantine's victory over Maxentius, but it would also have paved the way for the emperor to issue the Edict of Milan in 313 A.D. This decree did not, as is commonly supposed, make Christianity the state religion; rather, it proclaimed that Rome was to be neutral in religious matters. However, the Edict led to the ascendance of Christianity to its dominant position in the west over the next millennium.

The historian and Christian apologist Eusebius of Caesarea (260–339 A.D.) wrote a biography of Constantine, which was based, in part, on conversations he had with the emperor. According to Eusebius, Constantine resolved to go up against Maxentius because he felt Maxentius was tyrannizing Rome. Yet, he was concerned that his military power alone might not suffice to give him victory. Hence, during this period, he "sought Divine assistance, deeming the posses-sion of arms and a numerous soldiery of secondary importance, but believing the co-operating power of Deity invincible and not to be shaken" (1. 27). He prayed for a sign or confirmation, and on October 27, 312 A.D., at noon, was apparently granted one. It looked like a cross of light above the sun, with an inscription under it, reading, "By this sign, conquer." Constantine was uncertain about the vision but then had a clarifying dream that night when Christ himself appeared and told him to put the sign—the *chi rho* symbol, which superimposes the first two letters of Christ's name, in Greek—onto his men's shields. Constantine did so, and his army won the battle, which was partly fought on the Milvian Bridge (Figure 3.3).

Eusebius's reliability has often been called into question, partly be-cause he was working for the emperor when he wrote the biography and

Figure 3.3 Milvian Bridge (Ponte Milvio), Rome, Italy. The bridge is still used today for foot traffic. Photo by Livioandronico 2013. Wikimedia Commons.

because he openly advocated for Christianity. Yet he himself anticipates skepticism about the story when he admits that "the account [of the visions]... might have been hard to believe had it been related by any other person." However, he claims that Constantine himself shared it with him and "confirmed his statement by an oath" (1.28). Furthermore, Eusebius alleges that the ruler's entire army witnessed the sign as well. In addition, ... in the historian's eyes, the emperor's success in battle "established [the story's] truth" (1.28).

It is intriguing to consider what sky-sign, if any, was perceived by Constantine. The Abruzzo event is a possibility though, admittedly, the area is a significant distance from Rome, about 158 km (98 miles) away. And most meteors, better known as falling stars, appear for a very short period, often just a split second, and generally at night. However, on rare occasions, they can be sighted during the day, streaking across the sky, high enough to be seen for many miles around. Plus, this particular meteor—if meteor it was—would have had tremendous velocity when it blew up, and thus could have created a kind of mushroom cloud. Such clouds, produced by nuclear bombs, can be visible for up to 100 miles, even more. The U.S. military conducted a number of nuclear tests about 105 km (65 miles) northwest of Las Vegas in the 1950s, and the clouds produced by them appeared to spectators in Las Vegas. In addition, the flash of these explosions was evident as far away as Los Angeles (386 km/240 miles), as is shown in period photographs from L.A. and Las Vegas newspapers (Patowary par. 1).

On the other hand, in an influential 1993 article, historian Peter Weiss argues that the emperor saw a sundog, or parhelion, an optical effect that occurs when "sunlight refracts through hexagonal ice crystals that are oriented with their bases parallel to the horizon" (246). (The name stems from the fact that the resulting spots, which are on each side of the sun, appear to "dog" it.) There is a similar phenomenon called a "sun pillar," which occurs when "low angle-sunlight reflects off ice crystals in cirrus clouds" (Burnham and Dyer 67). Then again, meteorologist Robert Plant notes that "a rare event would be to combine" both sundog and pillar, the horizontal and vertical beams, respectively, "creating something which can indeed look like a cross." He notes that "this is not easily achieved, however," and cautions that "Rome around noon in late October is a most unlikely time and place to be able to catch it" (par. 9).

There is the additional challenge of explaining the inscription that the emperor supposedly saw in the heavens. Weiss suggests that Constantine was not claiming to see actual writing but instead referenced the inscription in order to explain the significance of his vision (247).

What light, if any, might the oral legends in this area shed on the question of a possible meteor strike in the Abruzzo? To answer this, we may consider excerpts from an account long preserved by members of the *superaequum* (Latin for "above the water"), a people-group who lived in the area until the Lombards dispersed them in the 6th century A.D. (Santilli et al. 316). There was once an active cult devoted to the god Dionysus here, which regularly celebrated with orgies and ecstatic reveling. One August, when the mountain snows had melted, the celebrants hiked up from the valley to the temple, and the festivities began as usual. This time, however, just when the celebration was in full swing, without warning, "an uproar hit the mountain and quartered the giant oaks announcing the arrival of the Goddess" (317). Presumably, this was Ariadne: Dionysus's wife.

The roar was followed by a wave of intense heat hitting the revelers, at which point "a shout echoed all around, splitting the air, with its trail of violence." As the votaries stared, what appeared to be a "new star, never seen before, came nearer and nearer." It was so bright it seemed like a second sun. Oak-leaves trembled and curled up, and the entire forest "lost its sap." The whole area "was shaking," and as the "star" shone, the sky radiated with its brilliance. Then, with a deafening crash, "the statue sank into a sudden chasm" (317).

The reference to a statue is puzzling, but it could be that the worshippers were registering, first, a shock wave from an incoming meteor, as Santilli et al. surmise (316), and then, possibly, a piece from the object crashing to the ground near them. In any case, when some time had passed, there was silence, and "men listened closely to the death rattle of the Goddess" (317). Then they saw a second statue, only this one, they believed, represented "the Madonna with the Holy Child in her arms who was sitting on a throne of light and was surrounded by light." In their eyes, "the Mother of God, carried here by the angels through the sky, had come to extirpate sin" (317). Possibly this second "statue," which may have been the main fireball, landed atop the first "pagan" one, crushing it, like Dorothy flattening the Wicked Witch of the East. This event stunned the roisterers, and they immediately converted to Christianity en masse. Eventually, a church was built on the site of the old pagan temple, with the statue itself placed on the altar.

Santilli et al. contend that "while this account clearly contains mythical elements and the narrative accretion of centuries, the description matches that of a meteorite falling in the [area] and the conversion to Christianity matches its date" (318). Hence, it would seem that geomythology played a role here, albeit a supporting one. The story of the descending "goddesses" does not confirm the meteor's existence, nor does the group conversion necessarily shed light on Constantine's individual transformation, yet the tale remains as a piece of evidence that can be assessed for future research on the alleged impact event.

People-Eating Birds?

Some sky-related legends feature not fiery explosions or plunging objects but rather massive birds that swoop down and carry off babies, children, and even, in some versions, full-grown men. Possibly the best-known myth here is that of Ganymede, the third son of the first king of Troy, who was reputedly so handsome that Zeus himself fell in love with him. Zeus then assumed the form of an eagle, flew down and spirited away the youth to serve as his cupbearer on Mt. Olympus. The story is told in Homer's *Iliad*, Book XX, and in the fifth book of Virgil's *Aeneid*.

Could the tale have been prompted by an actual episode? It seems unlikely, given that most eagles weigh 8–12 pounds and can only pick up about a 3–4 pound load (Woodford par. 2). Then again, eagles are relatively large raptors and have been known to lift cats, small dogs, and goats, so at least imagining a person getting picked up by one—especially if the bird were the incarnation of the head god—is not difficult. There is at least one modern episode that seems relevant, and it takes us back to Alice Springs, Australia. There, at a 2016 bird show, a boy was attacked by a wedge-tailed eagle. This is Australia's largest predatory bird, with wingspans of up to 7.5 feet, and has been seen raising small animals. Whether it was trying to do so here with the boy or simply to strike him is not clear. The attempt was unsuccessful, though the lad received a facial gash. In this case, experts claim, the bird was agitated by the boy, not necessarily looking for a meal—indeed, the birds in these shows are well-fed (Becker par. 6). Possibly, the young man's actions of moving his hoodie zipper up and down irritated the raptor (Becker pars. 8 and 9).

When we turn to Native American myths, there is a Yaqui legend that may be based on the appearances of massive condors in northwest Mexico (Mayor, "Fossil" 103). Today's condors have 10-foot wingspans and have been seen attacking deer. Their Pleistocene counterparts, whose nests have been discovered in caves, "contain the bones of mammoths, camels, bison, and horses, carried away as carrion" (104). These colossal birds, whose jaw-dropping size is reflected in their name *Teratornis incredibilis*, or teratorns, had wings measuring 17 feet; they certainly could have evoked such legends (Figure 3.4). They weighed 50+ pounds and had "long, strong hooked beaks for grabbing up prey." Mayor adds that this prey *"could have included humans"* (104; my emphasis). The bones of such creatures have been discovered throughout northern Mexico and the southern parts of the U.S. Their remains "almost always coexist with human occupation sites" (104), suggesting that the two species interacted, somehow.

Mayor also recounts a Hopi fable about a bird that abducts children, and in her study of First Nation myths, reproduces a photo of a petroglyph found in the Petrified National Forest (Arizona). This piece of art is about 600–1000 years old and seems to have been made by the ancestors of the Hopis: the Anasazis. It shows a startling image: a small man struggling in the beak of a massive bird (Mayor 164-65). Interestingly, the bird looks less like a raptor and closer to something like a crane. Instead of the hooked beak typical of a raptor, it has an extended, narrow one, more akin to that of, say, a sandhill crane, which has long been common in North America. Fossils of the birds dating up to 2.5 million years old have been found. Sandhills, moreover, have the small wings common to cranes, rather than the enormous ones typical of raptors.

Figure 3.4 Teratornis fossil. La Brea Tar Pits, Los Angeles, CA (USA). Photo by Funkmonk. Wikimedia Commons.

The petroglyph may represent another category of avian-human stories. In this case, what is involved are very large birds attacking, sometimes fatally, small humans such as pygmies or dwarves. The classic western reference here is in Homer's *Iliad,* Book III, which offers an epic simile. It likens the Trojans to cranes and the Greeks to pygmies:

> Now with the squadrons marshaled, captains leading each, the Trojans came with cries and the din of war like wildfowl when the long hoarse cries of cranes sweep on against the sky and the great formations flee from winter's grim ungodly storms, flying in force, shrieking south to the Ocean gulfs, speeding blood and death to the Pygmy warriors, launching at daybreak savage battle down upon their heads. (III. 1–7)

There are similar narratives in First Nation fables. Alex Scobie recounts four, from Cherokee, Nass, Comox, and Nisqually sources (126–27). In the first, some young Cherokee men encounter little people who are being terrorized by geese and other birds. The youths teach them how to use sticks for clubs and how to strike the birds with the implements. The little people successfully repel the birds—that is, "until a flock of sandhill cranes came" (126). Then, the narrator relates, "[the birds] were so tall that the little men could not reach up to strike them on the neck, and so at last the cranes killed them all" (126). In the second story, "birds come in great swarms" and kill many dwarves, who are then helped by a normal-sized man and his companions. The Comox and Nisqually versions are somewhat akin to the other two, and again, all four stories involve a battle between little people and birds.

Scobie argues that "these [native tales] might have arisen independently and need not be attributed to the influence of European settlers" (122). Instead, he contends, they could have been based, not on actual pygmies—there are none outside of Africa—but on dwarves, who feature in tales from South America (130). As for any potential truth informing crane-pygmy encounters, Scobie mentions some startling real-life examples from other areas of the world. One is from the *Oxford Classical Dictionary*, which refers to Aka pygmies, who are nomads based in the Central African Republic and the Republic of Congo (131 n.12). The OCD notes that "modern explorers [in these regions] report that the Aka dwarfs hunt cranes and that the birds vigorously resist" ("Pygmies"). The other is from the poet Statius (A.D. 45-96), cited earlier, who in his *Silvae* (1.6.57-64) reports the fascinating but grisly observation that the ancient Romans not only brought pygmies into the Roman Colosseum to fight like gladiators against one another but also that "cranes were provided ... to feed on the pygmies after they had killed each other" (Scobie 130, n.5).

Furthermore, we know that sandhill cranes are among the most aggressive of birds and do not hesitate to attack animals and people. Males can reach nearly five feet in height. Hunter-journalist Keith Sutton recounts his own hair-raising experiences with sandhills, especially their behavior, after he mistakenly assumed certain ones were already dead, apparently having been killed by hunters. In addition, he shares a story told by his hunting guide, Curt Wilkerson. After Wilkerson and one of the men he was working with had dispatched a few of the birds, they covered the bodies with a tarp. Moments later, as they walked away,

> Wilkerson heard a blood-curdling scream. He turned to see one of the [other] hunters trying to fight off an attacking crane. The man had the sandhill's neck in a death-grip, but again and again the bird buried its knifelike beak in his face. The talons of one foot were embedded in the man's arm; those of the other were locked in his thigh. Fortunately, the bird's thrusting bill missed his eyes, but the hunter was frightfully injured and had to be transported to a hospital. (Sutton, par. 31)

Based on such accounts, the legendary ones about crane-pygmy feuds seem quite believable.

"Killer" Lakes

On 21 August 1986, at about 9 p.m., residents living along Lake Nyos (Figure 3.5) in Cameroon (central west Africa) were winding down for the evening. Suddenly, a deafening explosion from the direction of the lake rocked the area. Within minutes, hundreds of people found themselves feeling intensely nauseous, while others passed out. The next morning, the local insects and birds, which would normally be buzzing and chirping, were weirdly silent. To their horror, villagers soon discovered hundreds of dead bodies, slain by some mysterious force. By the time the dead were counted, 1,746 people had perished, along with about 3,000 livestock and countless birds and insects. Some of the victims seemed to have died almost instantly; their corpses were discovered near cooking fires or in doorways (Krajick par. 6).

Scientists from around the world soon converged on the area to figure out what caused this small, picturesque lake to seemingly turn killer. One clue was a similar event from two years earlier when 37 people perished at Lake Monoun, about 60 miles south of Nyos. After that episode, researchers were uncertain about the cause. The Nyos disaster allowed them to connect the dots. They eventually realized that both events were extremely rare disasters called limnic eruptions or lake turnovers. Nyos is quite deep (682 feet) and is a crater lake. And because it is located in a volcanic region, the magma beneath the lake floor periodically releases certain gases, including carbon dioxide.

CO_2 is, of course, what we normally exhale and is also produced when we burn fossil fuels. In a lake such as Nyos, the CO_2 tends to

Figure 3.5 Lake Nyos, 29 August, 1986, two weeks after the disaster. U.S. Geological Survey. Wikimedia Commons.

remain on the lake bottom since it is denser and thus cannot mix with the water above (Black par. 13). Indeed, both Nyos and Monoun are what are called meromictic lakes; that is, they are "density stratified" (Tanyileke et al. 416); hence, their layers seldom mix or turn over. Most lakes, by contrast, are holomictic and do blend layers. In any event, the pressure from the CO_2 in meromictic lakes can be considerable, about 15 bars, compared to an unopened champagne bottle, which has about 5 bars. At some point, either on its own or jostled by a landslide or quake, the CO_2 can emerge suddenly, somewhat like a carbonated drink that is shaken and then opened. In the 1986 event, a noxious cloud, measuring an appalling billion cubic yards in size and traveling at about 45 mph, emerged, suffocating both humans and animals in minutes (Krajick par. 25).

These lakes are not the only ones associated with limnic eruptions. Lake Avernus, located near Naples, is an actual body of water that is mythologized in Virgil's *Aeneid*, and possibly in Dante's *Inferno*. In Book VI of the *Aeneid*, in order to access the underworld, Virgil enters Sibyl's cave, which is on Avernus. While the cave Dante enters at the beginning of the *Divine Comedy* is never named, it has been linked with Avernus as well. The name "Avernus" means "birdless" in Greek, and there are recorded instances, both in antiquity and in modern times, of the lake releasing poison gases and killing large numbers of fish and birds. In their 2008 study, Caliro et al. attributed one of these events, a 2005 fish kill, to the sudden overturn of toxic hydrogen sulfide gases on the lake bottom. The event was possibly triggered when shallower waters in Avernus cooled (the event occurred in February 2005), causing them to descend while the warmer, toxic layer rose to the surface (315).

Today, authorities are degassing Nyos and Monoun to prevent further catastrophes. The process has not always been a smooth one, yet a 2019 study by geoscientist Gregory Tanyileke et al. concluded that pipe installations in Lake Monoun in 2006 and in Nyos in 2011 have served to "accelerate the degassing" and have "worked well." Also worth noting is while the overturns at these lakes were horrific, a silver lining has emerged: both bodies of water "have become natural laboratories" for "the design and testing of new investigation methods and equipment and capacity building (infrastructural and human)" (416).

Still, there is at least one lake overturn waiting to happen. It could come from Lake Kivu, which borders Rwanda and the Democratic Republic of the Congo. Kivu is one of the African Great Lakes; others include Lake Victoria, Lake Malawi, and Lake Tanganyika. Combined, they contain more water than the North American Great Lakes. Kivu is some 17 times larger than Nyos and contains approximately 500 million tons of CO_2. Geologists estimate that an extinction event occurs at Kivu about every 3,000 years, presumably from a limnic eruption. Kivu thus appears to be a looming catastrophe, given its size and the fact that many people live on its shores. As for degassing it, such an operation would be quite costly and has thus not been carried out yet. Kivu has, therefore, earned the title of "the world's most dangerous lake."

Regarding Nyos, there are local legends and myths linked with it and with other lakes in the area. Anthropologist Eugenia Shanklin has studied these in detail. Prior to the 1986 explosion, she had been collecting stories about "misbehaving" lakes in the area for more than five years. These tales exhibited a variety of actions: sudden sinkage, precipitous rising, explosions, shifting of locations (overnight, at times), and color changes. Some of the older legends about Nyos suggest that "people around [it] have long been aware that the lake harbored destruction" (Krajick par. 10). Indeed, one ethnic group, the Bafmen, long believed in building on higher ground, "perhaps, in collective memory, as a defense against disaster" (par. 10). Ominously, the lake's name means "to crush" in the Itangikom language (par. 9), possibly alluding to some calamity. More recently, however, another people-group, the Fulani, began constructing housing lower down, closer to the water, and by the 1980s, the population around the lake was several thousand.

Shanklin notes that "there are 46 lakes in the Grassland region [where Nyos is located], a majority of which have ... legends recounting circumstances in which numbers of people ... were 'slaughtered' in or by the lake" (173). One of the earliest was recorded around 1913–15 by a Catholic missionary and concerned Lake Oku, which lies between Nyos and Monoun. While Oku did see the emergence of a waterspout in April 2011, it is larger and shallower than its two gas-active counterparts, and subsequent study of the waterspout by researchers determined that it was not caused by a limnic eruption (Tanyileke et al. 421). Yet, the legends linked to Oku are similar to those inspired by the other two. In one story, two rival groups, the Oku (who share a name with the lake) and the Kijem, were both approached by a stranger, asking if he might settle in the area. The Oku welcomed him while the Kijem spurned the man. When he eventually died, "his spirit-double went into the lake," and he invited leaders from both groups to join him. They did so, with the result that the Kijem leader died while the Oku one was rewarded (166). According to Shanklin, in one version, "the waters reddened with the blood of the Kijem leader" (166).

In the course of researching an article on the Nyos cataclysm, science journalist Kevin Krajick interviewed Ephriam Che, a local man whose people have lived on its shores for centuries. As they talked, Che related one tale passed down to him by his grandfather. In it, a number of settlers decided to cross Nyos, much like the Israelites traversed the Red Sea. When their Mosaic leader parted the waters, they entered the lake. However, in a detail that would be hilarious if it did not result in such terrible consequences, a mosquito suddenly bit their guide on one of his testicles. He quickly reached down to swat it, instantly losing control over the suspended waters. They immediately came roaring back, and the entire party was drowned (par. 11). Even so, according to Che, the ghosts of these unfortunates linger and at times can be heard by the living, talking amongst themselves. Here again, it is possible the tale preserves the memory of some real-life tragedy, though the presence of a live mosquito would seem to rule out the possibility of lake overturn.

Such legends are obviously regional since they are linked to particular lakes. Yet they raise the possibility that there have been similar events, not just in Africa and Italy, but other areas as well. Shanklin notes, for instance, that Celtic mythology "includes references to exploding lakes ... and lakes that misbehave spectacularly" (166). We may add that still other bodies, such as Lake Michigan (USA), function as natural CO_2 receptacles. In fact, Lake Michigan releases its store annually every November, though the discharge is spread out over a week's time, in contrast with the abrupt and deadly releases from Nyos and Monoun (Otto par. 12).

Even so, slower releases can have negative consequences. This fact points to a disheartening find by researchers: while lakes make up just 4% of the global land surface, nearly all of them, even the cleanest and purest, play a significant role in putting greenhouse gases into the atmosphere. This is because many plants end up in lakes after they die, having been brought there by rivers, rain, snow, and wind. At that point, microorganisms such as bacteria and fungi break the plants down. Since plants are organic, the microorganisms discharge carbon during this process. As Andrew Tanentzap notes, "as a byproduct of this never-ending feast, microbes release gases such as CO_2 and methane into the environment" (par. 5). He adds that sunlight also can cause decay in organic matter. As a result, "the amount of greenhouse gases released from lakes by microbes and sunlight is huge," around 25%, "over and above the Earth's carbon-storing processes" (par. 7).

More worrisome is that Tanentzap and his team estimate that this figure of 25% could double in the coming decades since climate change will cause most forests to become thicker. There will be an increase in tree cover resulting from higher numbers of maples and oaks, both of which have broad leaves. At the same time, pines and other needled trees will decline (par. 9). This increasingly abundant tree cover will mean that a higher amount of organic material will waft into lakes, eventually leading to more greenhouse gases being released into the atmosphere. In sum, it would appear that Nyos and Monoun, though extreme examples, are not outliers. Due to global warming, in a kind of human-induced slow violence, all lakes could eventually become killers.

4 The Futures of Geomythology

On December 26, 2004, the most devastating tsunami in recorded history formed in the Indian Ocean and soon wreaked havoc on parts of Thailand and Indonesia. Walls of water reaching nearly 100 feet in height tore through villages and towns, and when the waves finally receded, over 230,000 people had perished. The disaster was caused by a massive undersea earthquake registering around 9.2 and lasting longer (8–10 minutes) than any other quake in human memory.

In the midst of the mayhem and wreckage, one group survived against high odds. These were the Moken sea gypsies, who grow up on the sea and learn to swim before walking. Indeed, the name "Moken" means "people immersed in water." Journalist Susan Smillie notes that the Moken have a tale, passed down the generations around countless campfires, about a massive wave, or "laboon," which means "the people-eating wave." They are taught that when the "laboon" appears, they are to seek deeper water or flee to high ground. Because they did the former on that ghastly day in 2004, there were no casualties among the Moken—despite being, as Smillie puts it, "directly in the path of the ... wave" (par. 6).

Since then, the Moken have become known to the outside world as the "tsunami tribe," and unfortunately, their normally quiet corner of the world becomes overrun during tourist season, as bystanders gawk, snap endless pictures, and even, in some cases, try touching Moken for good luck (par. 6). Ironically, the Moken seem to have evaded one tragedy, only to fall victim to a more insidious one borne of consumerism and outsider greed. The latter fact is doubly regrettable, not only because of the ways the Moken are exploited post-tsunami but also because geotourism can constitute a legitimate growth area for geomythology. At its best, geotourism eschews mere profit for the nobler goals of promoting lay and scientific interest in the geological history of notable areas and by contributing to the preservation of these sites.

Khoshraftar and Farsani, for instance, argue that key geosites in Iran, including the Travertine Wall (Stone Dragon) and Solomon's Prison, "have geomythical value," since they were created when springs had lime deposited into their water, resulting in the travertine cones. (Travertine is a form of limestone formed by hot springs.) The colorful "explanations" for the sites allege that, in the first case, King Solomon petrified a colossal dragon with a mere command; in the second, that he confined a throng of malicious demons in the Prison, which looks like a small mountain (1883, 1884). While these explanations are clearly fanciful and after the fact, they may lay the foundation for geomythical study and promote conservation of these destinations (1887).

In any event, the story of the Moken's astonishing survival of the 2004 disaster is perhaps the most remarkable example of how geomyths can serve as first warning systems for geohazards. It also suggests another profitable avenue for future research. That is, geomyths can assist scientists and local communities in what Masse et al. call "hazard mitigation" (16) for events like tsunamis, quakes, and limnic eruptions. The stories can provide baselines against which more accurate preparations for future events can be carried out. For instance, Eugenia Shanklin's research, mentioned earlier, notes that "local folklore [in the Lake Nyos area] might be studied in more detail than has previously been the case, with particular attention to the features that prove deadly in local myth" (173). Thus, typical features in the legends of this area show that the explosions occur "in the rainy season and always at night" (173); hence, greater emergency preparedness could be increased during such times and conditions.

As noted in the introduction, geomythology has the potential to enrich literary theories such as trauma studies and ecocriticism. Yet, it can also spur the production of both literary and artistic work by inspiring writers and artists to compose new geomyths, either in response to cataclysms or to warn future generations of impending ones. Indeed, for certain perils such as nuclear waste, which poses a threat for many thousands of years in the future, the ability of myth to endure across times and cultures could prove invaluable, serving, say, to caution against digging in certain radioactive sites long after warnings in any current languages have morphed beyond recognition (Mayor, "Geomythology" 6).

In addition, a geomythology database or electronic archive containing both stories of geoevents and warnings for the future could be a worthy project, a site to which scholars and laypersons alike might contribute to pool geomythical knowledge. It could house various texts, including books, poems, songs, videos, scholarly articles, and artwork. There is at least one precursor, the CLEMENS database project, announced in 2007. The acronym stands for *Corpus Latinorum Et Mediaevalium Naturae Scriptorum* and would provide an "electronic archive of excerpta reporting environment-related data contained in the literary and epigraphic sources of classical and Roman Medieval age" (Vittori et al. 51).

Vitaliano and Mayor's works on geomyth could be an excellent foundation since both examine many such stories connected to Greek and Roman texts in their scholarship. Even a very cursory list would give scholars and laypersons alike a sense of the global scope of geomythology. One related resource is *Geowonderland*, a website that describes itself as "a land of places introduced through folktales and legends." This site is clearly meant for a non-scholarly audience and includes the Moken's laboon story, among others. Both *Geowonderland* and CLEMENS help to underscore the international perspective and worth of geomythology. Absent this outlook, it might be too easy to conclude that geomythology is a mere curiosity, limited to a relatively small number of stories from a handful of "primitive" cultures.

Moreover, geomythology could develop substantially as scholars read both canonical and non-canonical narratives afresh, searching for "new" geomyths. This would also be an enormous undertaking, given the sheer amount and variety of authors and sources, which range from high literary works such as Virgil's *Aeneid* to vernacular ones, and which include an array of western and non-western texts. Geomythology has tended to focus on oral tales, yet written ones are also important.

Mayor, as noted, has uncovered about 100 geomyths in Greek and Roman written narratives and Native American traditions ("First Fossil," "Fossil Legends"), and Barber and Barber have discovered geomythical resonances in Greek tales such as Prometheus, Python, and Minos. Van der Geer et al. have identified several in the *Mahābhārata* and other Indian sources, while Patrick Nunn has done similar work for aboriginal myth, both individually ("Ancient," "Edge") and collectively (Nunn et al.). My own work (Burbery "Fossil," "Geomythology") considers possible geomyths in Virgil's *Aeneid* and *Liber Monstrorum* (The Book of Monsters), a text with links to *Beowulf.* Many others await discovery. At the risk of sounding grandiose, we may be in a situation analogous to Georges Cuvier, the founder of paleontology, when he predicted (correctly) in the late 1790s that many more fossils would be unearthed in the coming decades (Kolbert 30), even though just a few had come to light at that point. Besides, it may well prove profitable to study pre-literate tribes throughout the world who are *presently* composing and telling new or relatively recent geomyths, as people-groups address climate change and the incursions of the outside world.

A related area that could be profitably engaged is cold, or at least lukewarm, cases from geomythical scholarship. These have not yet been fully solved, at least as much as any cases can be closed in this speculative discipline. For instance, as we saw in our second chapter, the bones that King Hygelac, Beowulf's king, are associated with, and which are described within the curious volume known as the *Liber Monstrorum*, might have belonged, in fact, to a mammoth or mastodon, whose remains were creatively misinterpreted (Burbery, "Fossil" 320). Whether the bones also affected the composition of the king's portrayal in *Beowulf* is not clear, but that question could be ascertained if further evidence emerges. In the previous chapter, we also noted the ongoing debate over the alleged impact craters in central Italy and whether the meteor that caused them affected Constantine's conversion.

Another unresolved crater debate has to do with the Greek legend of Phaethon. As the son of Apollo, he rashly seized the reins of his father's sun-chariot one day, then lost control of the vehicle, wreaking global havoc, and was finally brought down by one of Zeus's thunderbolts in a spectacular crash. A 2010 paper makes the case that the legend was inspired by a falling asteroid that plunged to earth around 2,500 years ago in what is now Bavaria (southeastern Germany) and constituted the foundation of the legend (Rappenglück et al.). The paper has received strong criticism (Doppler et al.), which was answered by the original authors.

Having reviewed the claims, petrologist Aley El-Shazly contended that "neither ... is 100% conclusive," and adds that "addressing the [remaining issues] should be fairly straightforward." To that end, he provided a list of key questions for future research: "Are there any shear zones [faults in which movement has taken place that is not marked by cracks or breaks] in the area that can be tied to these quartz fabrics and pseudotachylites [fine-grained rock formed by impact events]? Are there any minerals that can be dated (e.g., micas) along these shear zones? Are there any shatter cones [conical fractures resulting from a meteorite] or tektites?" He concludes on a hopeful note: "All that is needed is a bit more field work."

The claim also raises questions about the myth's origins and whether a narrative associated with a Greek deity and his son could have been inspired by an event that occurred some 1300 miles away in southern Germany. Potentially related here is the question of whether the Roman poet Ovid was acquainted with some version, perhaps exaggerated, of the event. His account of Phaethon's fall (in *Metamorphoses* II) greatly expands on Plato's *Timaeus*, in which Solon (an Athenian statesman) is told the story by an Egyptian priest. The priest notes, briefly, that upon losing control of his father's steeds, Phaethon set the entire earth ablaze. Ovid elaborates on this cursory mention and tells of whole cities set ablaze, as well as the earth splitting and cracking "in gaping fissures." Indeed, entire nations burn to the ground as Apollo's stallions run amok, unconstrained by Phaethon, and other nations are massively affected: Libya, for instance, then "became a desert," and Ethiopians, looking up at the debacle, straightaway "acquired their dark skin" (55–56).

Ovid's account of the youth's fall, especially its "explanations" of Ethiopian skin tone and Libya desertification, could sound like little more than an after-the-fact etiological geomyth. Yet in other ways it is reminiscent of a description of a comet or asteroid. Indeed, it cites an image of one: "Phaethon, with flames searing his glowing locks, was flung headlong, and went hurtling down through the air, leaving a long trail behind: just as sometimes a star, though it does not really fall, could yet be thought to fall from the clear sky" (58). It is, of course, entirely possible that the poet was simply employing an image he had seen himself, but it might also be that the story of the fall of a massive asteroid or comet had made its way down the centuries to him, as he composed the *Metamorphoses* in 8 A.D. If so, the original claim of the 2010 paper might be strengthened.

Also of interest are possible links between legends of bulls and earthquakes. As we saw in chapter 2, Krinitsky sees a possible allusion to a quake in the Bull of Heaven episode of the *Epic of Gilgamesh*, in which the animal splits open parts of the earth and drools on one of the epic's main characters. Similarly, Matt Kaplan, a paleontologist and science journalist, argues that the Minotaur, the notorious man-bull hybrid of myth, which lived underground as it awaited its victims, could have been inspired by the frequent powerful earthquakes in Crete ("Science of Monsters" 51–55). Kaplan has shown that tectonic activity during the alleged building of the labyrinth was especially high. Moreover, no remains of anything resembling a labyrinth in Crete were ever uncovered, even though the palace of the Cretan king, Minos, was, by archaeologist Sir Arthur Evans. It could be instructive to study this legend and other taurine narratives from literature and folklore from a geomythical perspective.

Indeed, such an undertaking is part of what could emerge as the field's most important contribution to science, which could occur when the tales begin driving the exploration, rather than merely confirming discoveries. Volcanologist Floyd McCoy argued in a 2009 article that the field's "next step ... is to reverse the current approach and start parsing old legends for clues to previously unrecognized events." Regarding this potential, McCoy enthuses, "it's like candyland" (qtd. in Lovett 38).

As discussed in chapter 3, astronomer Duane Hamacher has led the way here in his research on the aboriginal accounts of meteoric events in Australia. He has shown how such oral traditions anticipate Western findings of meteorites and craters (2). Also of note in this regard is a 2008 paper by geologist Donald A. Swanson. It focuses on the iconic Kīlauea volcano in Hawaii and the scandalous narrative it inspired about Pele and her sister. These tell of an intense episode involving Pele and her younger sister Hi'iaka. According to these traditions, when Pele first arrived in the Hawaiian Islands, accompanied by her sisters, she encountered a handsome man (Lohi'au), whom she soon desired. However, the island on which she found him (Kaua'i) was not suitable, so she worked her way southeast down the archipelago, finally coming to the largest island (Hawai'i) and settling in the Kilauea crater. She then asked Hi'iaka to bring Lohi'au to her, who agreed, on the condition that Pele refrain, for 40 days, from destroying a forest beloved by Hi'iaka. The bargain struck, Hi'iaka set off, only to be delayed past 40 days by many mishaps, including a hurricane. When she started back, she saw from afar that Pele had burnt the forest. Seething with revenge, Hi'iaka rushed home with Lohi'au, then marched to the top of Kīlauea. There, in full view of Pele, she and Lohi'au made love. Livid, Pele responded by slaying Lohi'au and hurling his body into the caldera, which caused Hi'iaka to dig frantically to recover him, though she was warned not to dig too deep, lest water quench Pele's fire. Rocks flew through the air, and eventually, Hi'iaka found her lover and resurrected him.

These narratives seem to have been inspired by Kīlauea's lava flow in the 15th century and, in the 16th century, the caldera's formation and its subsequent collapse (431). For instance, Swanson notes that the tale's detail about the desperate digging and airborne rocks "probably record explosions associated with the [caldera's] collapse, and the warning about water implies that the 'digging' reached substantial depth" (429). Notably, the details contradict previous geological studies, which posited that the caldera was formed considerably later, in a strong eruption in 1790. Yet Swanson argues that "Kīlauea's crater is both older than previous thought [by scientists] and the site of sporadic explosions during a 300-year period" (431), and notes that in this regard, "volcanologists were led astray by not paying close attention to the Hawaiian oral tradition" (430). He concludes that "[i]nterpretation of oral traditions is clearly important to understanding the past," serving both to confirm incomplete results, and importantly in terms of setting a research agenda, by *"providing ideas to pursue in the field"* (431; my emphasis). Swanson recognizes the challenges of doing so, given that "it is difficult to interpret anecdotes, particularly those cloaked in thick poetic metaphor" (430). Nevertheless, the effort can yield striking benefits, as in this study.

Until recently, myth-driven research has been the exception rather than the rule. Yet Hamacher and Swanson have pointed the way toward greater cooperation between myth and science and modeled ways that mythology can set the pace. Future research might start by examining bodies of legend and then ask whether the regions where the legends originate are known for, say, high levels of seismicity, volcanism, and/or rich fossil content. Such a two-pronged approach could yield significant discoveries and make geomythology an increasingly useful tool for science. And in the process, a bridge between science and the humanities might be strengthened.

Works Cited

Aksu, Ali E., Richard N. Hiscott, Peta J. Mudie, André Rochon, Michael A. Kaminski, Teofilo Abrajano, and Doan Yaar. "Persistent Holocene Outflow from the Black Sea to the Eastern Mediterranean Contradicts Noah's Flood Hypothesis." *GSA Today* 12.5 (2002): 1–10.

Alter, Robert. *The Five Books of Moses: A Translation with Commentary.* New York: W.W. Norton, 2004.

Axboe, Morton. "The Year 536 and the Scandinavian Gold Hoards." *Medieval Archaeology* 43 (1999): 186–188.

Baillie, M.G.L. "Dendrochronology Raises Questions About the Nature of the 536 AD Dust-Veil Event." *The Holocene* 4.2 (1994): 212–217.

Barber, Elizabeth Wayland, and Paul Barber. *When They Severed Earth from Sky: How the Human Mind Shapes Myth.* Princeton, New Jersey: Princeton UP, 2006.

Barras, Colin. "Is an Aboriginal Tale of an Ancient Volcano the Oldest Story Ever Told?" *Science/NAAS* 11 Feb. 2020.

Bate, Jonathan. "Living with the Weather." *Studies in Romanticism* 35 (1996): 431–447.

Becker, Rachel. "Why an Eagle Really Grabbed a Kid." *National Geographic.* 12 July 2016. Accessed 12 Nov. 2020.

Berger, W.H. "On The Extinction of the Mammoth: Science and Myth." *In Controversies in Modern Geology: Evolution of Geological Theories in Sedimentology, Earth History and Tectonics.* By D.W. Müller, J.A. McKenzie, and H. Weissert. London: Academic Press, 1991.

"Best of Sicily: A Land and Her People." http://www.bestofsicily.com/index.htm. n.d. Accessed 4 June 2020.

Birkerts, Sven. "On a Stanza by John Keats." In *Readings.* St. Paul, Minnesota: Graywolf, 1999: 174–186.

Black, Richard. "Action Needed on Deadly Lakes." *BBC News.* 27 Sept. 2005. Accessed 13 Aug. 2020.

Boer, Jelle Zeilinga de, and Donald T. Sanders. *Earthquakes in Human History: The Far-Reaching Effects of Seismic Disruptions.* Princeton, New Jersey: Princeton UP, 2007.

Boer, Jelle Zeilinga de, and Donald T. Sanders. *Volcanoes in Human History: The Far-Reaching Effects of Major Eruptions.* Princeton, New Jersey: Princeton UP, 2004.

Bondevik, S., S. Dawson, J. Mangerud, and A. Dawson. "Record-breaking Height for 8000-Year-Old Tsunami in the North Atlantic." *EOS, Transactions, American Geophysical Union* 84.31 (2003): 289–300.

Bressan, David. "Ancient Stories Preserve the Memory of Tsunami in the Pacific Ocean." *Forbes.* 23 March 2018. Accessed 4 June 2020.

Brönnimann S., and D. Krämer. "Tambora and the 'Year Without a Summer' of 1816. A Perspective on Earth and Human Systems Science." *Geographica Bernensia* G90 (2016): 48, doi:10.4480/GB2016.G90.01.

Buis, Alan. "Nope, Earth Isn't Cooling." *NASA Global Climate Change.* Blog post. 12 July 2019. Accessed 2 Dec. 2020.

Burbery, Timothy. "Fossil Folklore in the *Liber Monstrorum, Beowulf,* and Medieval Scholarship." *Folklore* 126.3 (Dec. 2015): 317–335.

Burbery, Timothy. "Geomythology and the Death of King Priam in *The Aeneid,* Book 2." *Folklore* 130.1 (March 2019): 81–88.

Burn, A.R. *Herodotus. The Histories,* ed. Trans. Aubrey de Sélincourt. London: Penguin Books, 1981.

Burnham, Robert, and Alan Dyer. *Practical Sky-Watching.* Petaluma, CA: Fog City Press, 2006.

Byock, Jesse. *Snorri Sturluson: The Prose Edda.* New York: Penguin Classics, 2005.

"California Earthquakes Expose Fossil 15 Million Years Old." *The Weather Channel.* 28 October 2019. Accessed 27 May 2020.

Caliro, S., G. Chiodini, G. Izzo, C. Minopoli, A. Signorini, R. Avino, and D. Granieri. "Geochemical and Biochemical Evidence of Lake Overturn and Fish Kill at Lake Averno, Italy." *Journal of Volcanology and Geothermal Research* 178 (2008): 305–316.

Campbell, Joseph. *The Hero with a Thousand Faces.* San Francisco, CA: New World Library, 2008.

Cimarelli, C., M. A. Alatorre-Ibargüengoitia, K. Aizawa, A. Yokoo, A. Díaz-Marina, M. Iguchi, and D. B. Dingwell. "Multiparametric Observation of Volcanic Lightning: Sakurajima Volcano, Japan." *Geophysical Research Letters* 43.9 (23 Feb. 2016). Accessed 20 Oct. 2020.

Clendenon, Cindy. *Hydrogeomythology and the Ancient Greek World: An Earth Science Perspective Emphasizing Karst Hydrology.* Lansing, Michigan: Fineline Science Press, 2009.

Cline, Eric H. *The Trojan War: A Very Short Introduction.* Oxford: Oxford UP, 2013.

Chinese Text Project. *Book of Changes,* "Qian." Trans. James Legge. https://ctext.org/book-of-changes/yi-jing?searchu=dragon.

Collins, Lorence. "Yes, Noah's Flood May Have Happened But Not Over the Whole Earth." *National Center for Science Education* 29.5 (Sept./Oct. 2009): 38–41.

Cruikshank, Julie. *Do Glaciers Listen?: Local Knowledge, Colonial Encounters, and Social Imagination.* Kindle ed., Vancouver, B.C.: UBC Press, 2014.

Cruikshank, Julie. "Oral Tradition and Oral History: Reviewing Some Issues." *Canadian Historical Review.* 75.3 (1994): 403–418.

Davis, Jim. "Glad You Asked: Do Ants Mine Gold?" *Utah Geological Survey.* May 2017. Accessed 20 Dec. 2020.

D'Huy, Julien. "Polyphemus: a Palaeolithic Tale?": The Retrospective Methods Network Newsletter, Department of Philosophy, History, Culture and Art Studies University of Helsinki, 2015: 43–64.

Doppler, Gerhard, Erwin Geiss, Ernst Kroemer, and Robert Traidl. "Response to 'The Fall of Phaethon: A Greco-Roman Geomyth Preserves the Memory of a Meteorite Impact in Bavaria (Southeastern Germany)' by Rappenglück, et al." *Antiquity* 8.327 (2011): 274–277.

Duggen, Svend, Peter Croot, Ulrike Schacht, and Linn Hoffmann. "Subduction Zone Volcanic Ash Can Fertilize the Surface Ocean and Stimulate Phytoplankton Growth: Evidence from Biogeochemical Experiments and Satellite Data." *Geophysical Research Letters* 34, 13 Jan. 2007: 1–5.

Durkheim, Emile. *The Elementary Forms of Religious Life.* Oxford: Oxford University Press, 2008.

Eagleton, Terry. *Literary Theory: An Introduction.* Minneapolis: University of Minnesota Press, 1983.

El-Shazly, Aley. "Re: Southern Germany Crater Theory." Email received by Timothy J. Burbery, 7 August 2020.

Eusebius of Caesarea. *The Life of the Blessed Emperor Constantine.* Trans. Ernest C. Richardson. Fordham University: Internet History Sourcebooks Project. Ed. Paul Halsall. Accessed 24 Dec. 2020.

Evans, K.J., and F.W. McCoy. "Precursory Eruptive Activity and Implied Cultural Responses to the Late Bronze Age (LBA) Eruption of Thera (Santorini, Greece)." *Journal of Volcanology and Geothermal Research* 397 (2020): 1–8.

Fine, Elisha, and Steven Fine. "Rabbinic Paleontology: Jewish Encounters with Fossil Giants in Roman Antiquity." Forthcoming in *Land and Spirituality in Rabbinic Thought.* Ed. S. Schick. London: Brill, 2021.

"Florida Man Swallowed by Sinkhole under Bedroom Feared Dead." *The Guardian.* 1 March 2013. Accessed 2 June 2020.

Galanopoulos, Angelos. "Die ägyptischen Plagen und der Auszug Israels aus geologischer Sicht." *Das Altertum* 10 (1964): 131–137.

Geer, Alexandra. van der et al. "Fossil Folklore from India: The Siwalik Hills and the *Mahābhārata.*" *Folklore* 119 (2000): 71–92.

Gilgamesh: A New English Version. Trans. Stephen Mitchell. New York, London: Free Press, 2004.

Glenn, Justin. "The Polyphemus Myth: Its Origin and Interpretation." *Greece and Rome* 25.2 (1978): 141–155.

Glotfelty, Cheryll. "Introduction." In Cheryll Glotfelty and Harold Fromm, eds. *The Ecocriticism Reader: Landmarks in Literary Ecology.* Atlanta, Georgia: University of Georgia Press, 1996: xv–xxxvii.

Gräslund, B., and Neil Price. "Twilight of the Gods?: The 'Dust Veil Event' of AD 536 in Critical Perspective." *Antiquity* 86.332 (2012): 428–443.

Greene, Mott. *Natural Knowledge in Preclassical Antiquity.* Baltimore, London: Johns Hopkins University Press, 1992.

Hanfmann, George M.A. "Pygmies." In *Oxford Classical Dictionary.* N.G.L. Hammon and H.H. Sculland, eds. 2nd edition. Oxford: Oxford UP, 1970.

Hamacher, Duane W. "Recorded Accounts of Meteoritic Events in the Oral Traditions of Indigenous Australians." *Archaeoastronomy: The Journal of Astronomy in Culture* 25 (2014): 1–16.

Harris, W.V. *The Ancient Mediterranean Environment between Science and History.* London: Brill Publishing, 2013.

Hartzman, Marc. "Cyclops Baby Born in India Only Survives 1 Day." *AOL News.* 24 March 2011. Accessed 6 June 2020.

Hesiod. *The Theogony of Hesiod.* Trans. Hugh G. Evelyn-White. Mineola, NY: Dover Publications, 1914.

Hill, Carol A. "The Noachian Flood: Universal or Local?" *Perspectives on Science and Christian Faith* 54 (2002): 170–183.

Homer: The Iliad. Trans. Robert Fagles. New York: Penguin, 1997.

Homer: The Odyssey. Trans. Robert Fagles. New York: Penguin, 1997.

Honko, Lauri. "The Problem of Defining Myth." In *Sacred Narrative: Readings in the Theory of Myth.* Ed. Alan Dundes. Berkeley, CA: University of California Press, 1984: 41–52.

Hunter, Dana. "The Underappreciated Threat of Volcanic Tsunamis." *Scientific American.* 19 Mar. 2019. Accessed 24 Oct. 2020.

Iyengar, R.N., and B.P. Radhakrishna. "Evolution of the Western Coastline of India and the Probable Location of Dwārakā of Kr.s.n.a: Geological Perspectives." *Journal of the Geological Society of India* 66 (Sept. 2005): 285–292.

Jaynes, Julian. *The Origin of Consciousness in the Breakdown of the Bicameral Mind.* New York: Houghton-Mifflin, 1990.

Josephson-Storm, Jason. *The Myth of Disenchantment: Magic, Modernity, and the Birth of the Human Sciences.* Chicago: University of Chicago Press, 2017.

Kaiser, Walter C., and Duane A. Garrett. *New International Archaeological Study Bible: An Illustrated Walk through Biblical History and Culture.* Grand Rapids, Michigan: Zondervan, 2005.

Kaplan, Matt. *Science of the Magical: From the Holy Grail to Love Potions to Superpowers.* New York: Scribner, 2015.

Kaplan, Matt. *The Science of Monsters: The Origins of the Creatures We Love to Fear.* New York: Scribner, 2013.

Khoshraftar, Reza, and Neda Torabi Farsani. "Geomythology: An Approach for Attracting Geotourists." *Geoheritage* 11 (2019): 1879–1888.

Kidner, Derek. *Genesis: An Introduction and Commentary.* Downer's Grove, Illinois: Inter-Varsity Press, 2019.

King, Darren N., Wendy S. Shaw, Peter N. Meihana, and James R. Goff. "Maori Oral Histories and the Impact of Tsunamis in Aotearoa-New Zealand." *Natural Hazards and Earth Systems Sciences* 18 (2018): 909–918.

Kirk, G.S. *Myth: Its Meanings & Functions in Ancient & Other Cultures.* Berkeley, California: University of California Press, 1973.

Kolbert, Elizabeth. *The Sixth Extinction: An Unnatural History.* London: Picador, 2015.

Krajick, Kevin. "Defusing Africa's Killer Lakes." *Smithsonian* 34.6 (Sept. 2003). Accessed 25 Oct. 2020.

Krinitzsky, Ellis L. "Earthquakes and soil liquefaction in flood stories of the ancient Near East." *Engineering Geology* 76 (2005): 295–311.

Lacovara, Kenneth. *Why Dinosaurs Matter.* New York: Simon and Schuster, 2017.
L. B. Larsen B. M. Vinther K. R. Briffa T. M. Melvin H. B. Clausen P. D.
    Jones M.-L. Siggaard-Andersen C. U. Hammer M. Eronen H. Grudd B.
    E. Gunnarson R. M. Hantemirov M. M. Naurzbaev K. Nicolussi. "New
    Ice Core Evidence for a Volcanic Cause of the A.D. 536 Dust Veil."
    Geophysical Research Letters 35 (2008): 1–5.
Laughead, William B. *The Marvelous Exploits of Paul Bunyan.* Minneapolis,
    Minnesota: Red River Lumber Company, 1916.
Liviu, Giosan, Florin Filip, and Stefan Constatinescu. "Was the Black Sea
    Catastrophically Flooded in the Early Holocene?" *Quaternary Science
    Reviews* 28 (2009): 1–6.
Lord, Albert B. *The Singer of Tales.* 2nd edition. Stephen Mitchell and Gregory
    Nagy, eds. Cambridge, Massachusetts: Harvard University Press, 2003.
Lovett, Richard A. "From Atlantis to Canoe-Eating Trees: Geomythology
    Comes of Age." *Analog Science Fiction & Fact* 129.9.9. (Sept. 2009): 32–38.
Marshak, Stephen. *EARTH: Portrait of a Planet.* New York, London: W.W.
    Norton, 2015.
Masse, W. Bruce, Elizabeth Wayland Barber, Paul T. Barber, and Luigi
    Piccardi. "Exploring the Nature of Myth and Its Role in Science." In *Myth
    and Geology.* Eds. L. Piccardi and W.B. Masse. Geological Society, London,
    Special Publications, 273, 2007: 9–28.
Mayor, Adrienne. "Ancient Fossil Discoveries and Interpretations." In *The
    Oxford Handbook of Animals in Classical Thought and Life.* Ed. Gordon L.
    Campbell. Oxford Handbooks Online. Oxford University Press, 2018: 579–588.
Mayor, Adrienne. *Fossil Legends of the First Americans.* Princeton, New
    Jersey: Princeton University Press, 2005.
Mayor, Adrienne. "Geomythology." *Encyclopedia of Geology.* Ed. Richard
    Selley, et al. Elsevier, 2005. https://www.sciencedirect.com/referencework/
    9780123693969/encyclopedia-of-geology.
Mayor, Adrienne. "Slaves First Identified Elephant Fossils in America."
    Wonders & Marvels. n.d. http://www.wondersandmarvels.com/2014/04/
    who-first-identified-elephant-fossils-in-america.html
Mayor, Adrienne. *The First Fossil-Hunters: Dinosaurs, Mammoths, and Myth
    in Greek and Roman Times.* 2nd ed. Princeton, New Jersey: Princeton
    University Press, 2011.
Montgomery, David. "A Geologist's Investigation into Noah's Flood." TED.
    2012. Lecture.
Montgomery, David. *The Rocks Don't Lie: A Geologist Investigates Noah's
    Flood.* New York: W.W. Norton, 2013.
Nelson, Edward. "The One-Eyed Ones." *Journal of American Folklore* 71
    (1958): 159–161.
Nunn, Patrick D. "Ancient Aboriginal Stories Preserve History of a Rise in
    Sea Level." *The Conversation.* 12 Jan. 2015.
Nunn, Patrick D. *The Edge of Memory: Ancient Stories, Oral Tradition, and
    the Post-Glacial World.* Kindle ed. New York: Bloomsbury/Sigma, 2018.
Nunn, Patrick D., Tony Heorake, Eshter Tegu, Bronwyn Oloni, Kellington
    Simeon, Lysa Wini, Sereana Usuramo, and Paul Geraghty. "Geohazards

Revealed by Myths in the Pacific: A Study of Islands that Have Disappeared in the Solomon Islands." *South Pacific Studies* 27.1 (2006): 1–49.

Nur, Amos, with Dawn Burgess. *Apocalypse: Earthquakes, Archaeology, and the Wrath of God.* Princeton, New Jersey: Princeton UP, 2008.

Ogden, Daniel. "Dragonscapes and Dread." In *Landscapes of Dread in Classical Antiquity: Negative Emotion in Natural and Constructed Spaces.* Ed. Debbie Felton. New York: Routledge, 2018: 165–184.

Otto, Laura. "When Lake Michigan Burps." *University of Wisconsin at Milwaukee/School of Freshwater Sciences.* Accessed 24 Nov. 2020.

Ovid. *Metamorphoses*: Translation and introduction by. Mary M. Innes. London: Penguin Books, 1983.

Panagiotakopulu, Eva, Thomas Higham, A. Sarpaki, and Paul C. Buckland. "Ancient Pests: The Season of the Santorini Minoan Volcanic Eruption and a Date from Insect Chitin." *The Science of Nature.* 22 May 2013. Accessed 28 May 2020.

Patowary, Kaushik. "How the Atomic Tests Looked Like from Los Angeles." *Amusing Planet.* 9 Sept. 2016. Accessed 10 Oct. 2020.

Pearson, Charlotte L., Darren S. Dale, Peter W. Brewer, Peter I. Kuniholm, Jeffrey Lipton, and Sturt W. Manning. "Dendrochemical Analysis of a Tree-ring Growth Anomaly Associated with the Late Bronze Age Eruption of Thera." *Journal of Archaeological Science* 36 (2009): 1206–1214.

Peek, Katie. "The Elusive Northwest Passage." *Scientific American* 316.5 (May 2017): 80.

Peissel, Michel. *The Ants' Gold: The Discovery of the Greek El Dorado in the Himalayas.* New York: Collins, 1984.

Piccardi, Luigi, and W.B. Masse, eds. *Myth and Geology.* London: Geological Society Special Publication 273, 2007.

Plant, Robert. "When Meteorology Altered the Course of History (or Maybe Not)." *Weather and Climate @Reading.* Blog post. 14 Nov. 2016. Accessed 8 Aug. 2020.

Rao, S.R. "Further Excavations of the Submerged City of Dwarka." Recent Advances in Marine Archaeology: Proceedings of the second Indian Conference on Marine Archaeology of Indian Ocean Countries, January 1990. *Marine Archaeology.* National Institute of Oceanography: 51–59.

Rappenglück, Barbara, Michael A. Rappenglück, Kord Ernstson, Werner Mayer, Andreas Neumair, Dirk Sudhaus, and Ioannis Liritzis. "The Fall of Phaethon: A Greco-Roman Geomyth Preserves the Memory of a Meteorite Impact in Bavaria (South-east Germany)." *Antiquity* 84.324 (2010): 438–439.

Reimer, Thomas. "Larger Than Foxes — But Smaller Than Dogs: The Gold-Digging Ants of Herodotus." *Reinardus* 19 (2006): 167–178.

Riordan, Rick. *The Battle of the Labyrinth.* New York: Hyperion Books, 2008.

Ryan, William B.F. and Walter Pitman. *Noah's Flood: The New Scientific Discoveries about the Event that Changed History.* New York: Simon & Schuster, 2000.

Ryan, William, Walter Pitman III, Candace O. Major, Kazimieras Shimkus, Vladamir Moskalenko, Glenn A. Jones, Petko Dimitrov, Naci Gorür,

Mehmet Sakinc, and Hüseyin Yüce. "An Abrupt Drowning of the Black Sea Shelf." *Marine Geology* 138 (1997): 119–126.
Santilli, Robert, Jens Ormo, Angelo R. Rossi, and Goro Komatsu. "A Catastrophe Remembered: A Meteorite Impact of the Fifth Century A.D. in the Abruzzo, Central Italy." *Antiquity* 77.296 (June 2003): 313–320.
Schneider, David. "It Came from Outer Space?" *The American Scientist* 92.6 (Nov/Dec 2004): 510–511.
Scobie, Alex. "The Battle of the Pygmies and the Cranes in Chinese, Arab, and North American Indian Sources." *Folklore* 86.2 (1975): 122–132.
Selley, Richard C., L.R.M. Cocks, and Ian R. Plimer, eds. *Encyclopedia of Geology*. New York: Elsevier, 2005.
Shanklin, Eugenia. "Exploding Lakes in Myth and Reality: An African Case Study." In *Myth and Geology*. Eds. L. Piccardi and W.B. Masse. Geological Society, London, Special Publications, 273, 2007: 165–176.
Shippey, Tom. *The Road to Middle-earth: How J.R.R. Tolkien Created a New Mythology*. New York: Houghton-Mifflin, 2003.
Sikemma, Doug. "Disenchantment, Actually." *The New Atlantis* 97 (2018): 96–103. https://www.thenewatlantis.com/publications/disenchantment-actually.
Sigl, M. Winstrup, M. McConnell, J. R. Welten, K. C. Plunkett, G. Ludlow, F. Büntgen, U. Caffee, M. Chellman, N. Dahl-Jensen, D. Fischer, H. Kipfstuhl, S. Kostick, C. Maselli, O. J. Mekhaldi, F. Mulvaney, R. Muscheler, R. Pasteris, D. R. Pilcher, J. R. Salzer, M. Schüpbach, S. Steffensen, J. P. Vinther, B. M. & Woodruff, T. E. "Timing and climate forcing of volcanic eruptions for the past 2,500 years." *Nature* 523 543–549 (2015). https://doi.org/10.1038/nature14565.
Simons, Marlise. "Himalayas Offer Clue to Legend of Gold-Digging 'Ants.'" *The New York Times*, 25 Nov. 1996. Interview with Michel Peissel. Accessed 23 Dec. 2020.
Sivertsen, Barbara J. *The Parting of the Sea: How Volcanoes, Earthquakes, and Plagues Shaped the Story of Exodus*. Princeton, New Jersey: Princeton UP, 2009.
Smillie, Susan. *The Last Sea Nomads: Inside the Disappearing World of the Moken*. Kindle ed., London: The Guardian, 2014.
Smith, Kimberly E. "Revisiting Tunguska: 111-Year-Old Mystery Impact Inspires New, More Optimistic Asteroid Projections." *NASA*. 26 June 2019. Accessed 23 Dec. 2020.
Starr, Michelle. "A Devastating Geologic Event in Indonesia May Have Helped Defeat Napoleon." *Science Alert*. 24 Aug. 2018. Accessed 28 Dec. 2020.
Statius. *Thebaid*. Trans. J.H. Mozley. Loeb Classics. Cambridge, Massachusetts: Harvard University Press, 1928.
Sutton, Keith. "The World's Most Dangerous Gamebird?" *Arkansas Democrat Gazette*, 1 Dec. 2013. Accessed 2 March 2020.
Swanson, Donald A. "Hawaiian Oral Tradition Describes 400 Years of Volcanic Activity at Kīlauea." *Journal of Volcanology and Geothermal Research* 176 (2008): 427–431.
Tanentzap, Andrew. "Freshwater Lakes Already Emit a Quarter of Global Carbon—and Climate Change Could Double That." *The Conversation*. 19 Nov. 2019. Accessed 3 Nov. 2020.

Tanyileke, Gregory, Romaric Ntchantcho, Wilson Yetoh Fantong, Festus Tongwa Aka, and Joseph Victor Hell. "30 years of the Lakes Nyos and Monoun gas disasters: A scientific, technological, institutional and social adventure." *Journal of African Earth Sciences.* 150 (2019): 415–424.

"The 11 Biggest Volcanic Eruptions in History." *LIVE SCIENCE.* 23 Feb. 2016. Accessed 10 Dec. 2020.

Thucydides. *The Peloponnesian War.* Trans. Rex Warner. New York: Penguin, 1977: 409.

Tigay, Jeffrey H. *The Evolution of the Gilgamesh Epic.* Philadelphia, PA: University of Pennsylvania Press, 1982.

Torrese, A.P., J. Rossi, M.L. Ormo, and G.G. Ori Rainone. "Investigating the Subsurface Structure of the Main Crater of the Proposed Sirente Meteorite Crater Field (Central Italy): New Clues from Reflection Seismics." *Planetary and Space Science 2018* 168 (2019): 27–39.

Virgil. *The Aeneid.* Trans. Robert Fitzgerald. New York: Random House, 1983.

Vitaliano, Dorothy. *Legends of the Earth: Their Geologic Origins.* Bloomington, Indiana: Indiana University Press, 1973.

Vittori, Eutizio, et al. "Environmental and Natural Hazards in Roman and Medieval Texts: Presentation of the CLEMENS Database Project." In *Myth and Geology.* Eds. L. Piccardi and W.B. Masse. Geological Society, London, Special Publications, 273, 2007: 51–59.

Webb, Richard. "Brexit: 10,000 years B.C.: The Untold Story of How Britain First Left Europe." *New Scientist.* 6 March 2019. Accessed 4 June 2020.

Weiss, Peter. "The Vision of Constantine." *Journal of Roman Archaeology* 16 (2003): 237–257.

Wood, Gillen D. "Largest Volcanic Eruption in Human History Changed the 19th Century as much as Napoleon." *The Conversation.* 7 Apr. 2014. Accessed 21 Dec. 2020.

Woodford, Riley. "Eagle Flight and Other Myths: Eagles Don't Eat Children or Pets." *Alaska Fish & Wildlife News.* Jan. 2008. Accessed 23 Sept. 2019.

Xing, Lida, Adrienne Mayor, Yu Chen, Jerald D. Harris, and Michael E. Burns. "The Folklore of Dinosaur Trackways in China: Impact on Paleontology." *Ichnos* 18 (2011): 213–220.

Yanchilina, Anastasia G., William B.F. Ryan, Jerry F. McManus, Petko Dimitrov, Dimitar Dmitrov, Krasimira Slovova, and Mariana Filipova-Marinova. "Compilations of Geophysical, Geochronological, and Geochemical Evidence Indicates a Rapid Mediterranean-derived Submergence of the Black Sea's Shelf and Subsequent Substantial Salinification in the Early Holocene." *Marine Geology* 383 (2017): 14–34.

Zielinski, Sarah. "To Find Meteorites, Listen to the Legends of Australian Aborigines." *Smithsonian Magazine.* 3 Oct. 2014. Accessed 6 June 2020.

Index

Note: *Italicized* page numbers refer to figures

For Product Safety Concerns and Information please contact our EU
representative GPSR@taylorandfrancis.com
Taylor & Francis Verlag GmbH, Kaufingerstraße 24, 80331 München, Germany

www.ingramcontent.com/pod-product-compliance
Lightning Source LLC
Chambersburg PA
CBHW071054280326
41928CB00050B/2507